D0183820

# wagamama

*ways with noodles*

Hugo Arnold

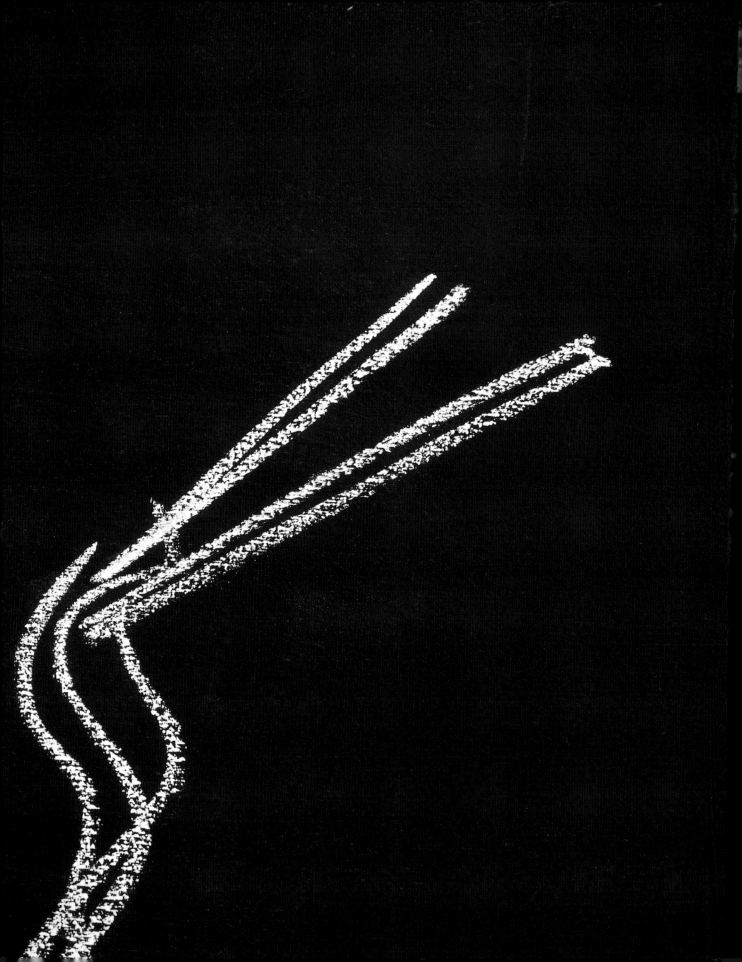

# wagamama

## ways with noodles

Hugo Arnold

**Author** Hugo Arnold    **Project editor** Jennifer Wheatley    **Photographer** Ditte Isager    **Art direction and design**    Lucy Gowans
**Food stylist** Jacque Malouf    **Props stylist** Tabitha Hawkins    **Copy editor** Stephanie Evans    **Editorial assistant** Vicki Murrell
**Production** Sha Huxtable and Alice Holloway

First published in Great Britain in 2006 by Kyle Cathie Limited, 122 Arlington Road, London NW1 7HP
general.enquiries@kyle-cathie.com   www.kylecathie.com

ISBN 1 85626 646 X     ISBN (13-digit) 978 1 85626 646 8

All rights reserved. No reproduction, copy or transmission of this publication may be made without written permission. No paragraph of this publication
may be reproduced, copied or transmitted save with written permission or in accordance with the provision of the Copyright Act 1956 (as amended).
Any person who does any unauthorised act in relation to this publication may be liable to criminal prosecution and civil claims for damages.

Text © 2006 wagamama limited
Photography © 2006 wagamama limited
'Girl & bowl' photograph (appears on p24, p64 and p189) © Judah Passow

wagamama and positive eating + positive living are registered trademarks of wagamama limited

Hugo Arnold is hereby identified as the author of this work in accordance with Section 77 of the Copyright, Designs and Patents Act 1988

A CIP catalogue record for this book is available from the British Library

Colour separations by Sang Choy, Singapore
Printed and bound in Singapore by Tien Wah Press

*Recipe photographs refer to the first recipe featured on the facing page*

# contents

# noodles, topping, broth…

this is where we started.

it defines what wagamama is all about.

a bench. a bowl. nutritious food.

speedy service. satisfaction. simplicity.

We are wild about noodles. Sure we do rice dishes – and adore them too – but noodles are what really get us going. wagamama may be known for *ramen*, but our enthusiasm doesn't stop there; stir fries, salads, quick ones, child-friendly ones. There really is no end to the variations.

Noodles epitomise fast food. They are easy to prepare and utterly versatile. It might be *ramen* or soup tonight, stir fry tomorrow and the next night something more like a stew. We like to call these one-pots. The topping might be meat or fish or vegetables – sometimes a combination of all three.

Cooking noodles is simple. They are invariably softened in boiling unsalted water, refreshed under cold water then combined with other ingredients. Which also makes them fast. And easy to control. If you like more chilli, less ginger or lots of garlic it is easy to dress your noodles accordingly. Or not at all. Some people like to dip their noodles in sauce, and why not?

You may like a thick noodle, or a thin one. It is up to you to choose. We have some rules, but they are not very strict. You may not be able to make a *gyoza* out of a strip of *udon* noodle, but there is nothing wrong with substituting *ramen* for *somen*, if that is what you prefer.

Noodles have been eaten for centuries and while the debate continues over whether noodles or pasta came first, we like to keep

East. It is something about the soy and ginger, the fresh mint and greens that we find hard to resist. One bowl containing these ingredients is enough to refresh and invigorate, soothe and comfort.

Whereas Italy seeks variety through shape, Asia provides interest through type: egg, rice, wheat, buckwheat, beanthread and potato. Uses vary, but as with any cuisine there are preferred partners and techniques (see pages 8–9). Noodles provide infinite combinations of taste, texture and flavour, given the various starches they contain. They partner with ease, never complaining, always willing. Try beef with black beans and egg noodles then the next time with rice noodles. You may have a preference (we certainly do), but both work equally well. As do egg or buckwheat noodles in spiced duck, asparagus and noodle soup (along with a healthy dose of soy, coriander and toasted sesame seeds).

Noodles are central to Asian cuisine. They stretch through Japan, Korea, China, Vietnam, Thailand, Malaysia and into Indonesia, turning up in soups, side dishes, as nests or packaging for meat, fish or vegetables, as beds for curry or in a salad. They can be stir fried or dressed, or poached in a heady broth, with aromatics provided by freshly chopped herbs.

Add convenience to this versatility. Most noodles have a shelf-life of at least a few weeks – longer if they are dried. They are inexpensive, easy to cook and nutritious. No wonder they are found in such diverse settings as remote mountain villages in China, downtown Tokyo and the beaches of Thailand.

Noodles are the fast food of today. You can stir fry in minutes, conjure a broth in less time than it takes to make a cup of tea, even fashion a salad in mere moments. And they are nothing if not healthy: high in complex carbohydrates, low in fat and essentially free from additives, while most if not all recipes make much use of fresh vegetables. The emphasis on fish and only a small quantity of meat is in keeping with dietary advice of the 21st century.

At wagamama noodles are a way of life: fun – sexy, even. Slurping noodles is one of those simple pleasures. The sort that leaves you with a smile of satisfaction. In our restaurants we encourage the slurping, a practice that is considered proper in Japan. Whether you want to slurp at home is entirely up to you but these recipes provide ample opportunity whichever way you decide to go.

# noodle knowledge

Noodles excel in a soup and get dressed in a sauce with real style. They come hot. They come cold. They are dipped in sauces, deep fried, wrapped and, on occasion, are fashioned into nests for other ingredients. They come fat and thin, and are made from rice, wheat, and even beans and potatoes. They are quick, versatile and healthy – a perfect food in many ways. They also calm and restore. And excite.

At wagamama we use the word *ramen*, which refers to the noodle, but also to the bowl where the noodle is combined with broth and vegetables and often fish or meat. Sometimes it may include all of these ingredients – as in wagamama *ramen*, a dish that we are rather proud of. *Ramen* is pretty key at wagamama. Served at noodle stalls thoughout Asia this hot, fresh, tasty, near-instant food is what started the wagamama way.

Noodles are very like pasta. Their shape is not crucial, but it does help. How you cook them is important too. In a *ramen* you want the starch in the noodle to combine with the broth. In a dish where the noodle is dressed, you want the starch inside the noodle to stay there. That way the dressing sticks and everyone is happy. Including the noodle.

Noodles have soul; they need to be handled carefully. Not timidly, but with respect. Noodles don't like salted water for example. The seasoning should happen in the dish. It's just their way. Some like to be boiled, others are happy in hot water. Almost all like to be precooked, which makes your job so much easier. And quicker.

You can be neat and tidy with noodles, but it's much more fun not to be. At wagamama we like to slurp – it feels more relaxed. What's more, the oxygen enhances their flavour. We are often asked how we decide on which noodle to use. The answer is not easy. We could say it doesn't matter too much. But it does. Sort of.

**Rice ones (1)** Often called rice-stick noodles, but also vermicelli. The difference is thin or really thin. The latter only require soaking in hot water to soften and are then used in salads, soups and stir fries. Rice-stick noodles, or 'sticks', as they are known, come as medium and wide. If this sounds a little confusing it is, not helped by each noodle company seemingly at odds over what is medium and wide. There are also the really wide ones, which are used in stir fries. Rice noodles tend to suit lighter dishes such as those with a broth rather than a heavy sauce. Gluten-free and wheat-free, they are usually sold dried, in nests.

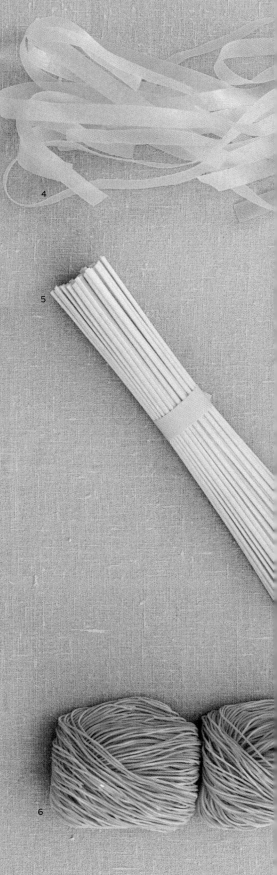

**Wrapping ones (2)** Some call them wontons, we call them *gyozas*. But they all amount to the same thing: wrappers. You might call them sandwiches, but that would be missing the point. These are generally rather more delicate – a thin skin covering anything from meat to fish to vegetables and even noodles (see the slippery ones below). You can bake, steam, deep fry or boil these noodles according to your mood, or to what stuffing you are using. Wrappers come in wheat and rice versions and are also known as spring roll wrappers. Buy fresh or frozen.

**Bucking ones (3)** Buckwheat lends a brown-grey colour to noodles, and a wonderful nutty flavour. In Korea they call them *naengmyon;* in Japan they are known as *soba*. These noodles are often served cold, and are dipped in sauces for breakfast in Japan. But they also turn up in soups. There are some who think *soba* noodles work in salads, but they need careful handling. They need lots of other ingredients and a good dressing or they can show up too worthy, too healthy by far. We are all for healthy eating. But it should be fun too. Buckwheat noodles are usually sold dried and the 100 per cent buckwheat version have the virtue of being gluten-free and wheat-free.

**Slippery ones (4)** Often referred to as cellophane noodles, but also as beanthreads, these crunchy, slippery, translucent, gelatinous strands deliver little in the way of flavour but bags of texture. The trick is to get the typically light sauce to coat each strand, that way they perform as noodles (lumps are not a good thing when it comes to noodles). Also fantastic in salads, cellophane noodles are sold dried.

**Wheaty ones (5)** The richness of egg noodles is not always what you are looking for, particularly when the other ingredients are high in the protein stakes. Wheat noodles are said to be the oldest form of Chinese noodle, and have a firm but somewhat silky bite. In their thin form (*somen*) they find their way into soups. The thicker version (*udon*) gets dressed in rich dishes where the heart and soul is as much in the sauce as the other ingredients. *Udon* noodles are fat, white, unctuous, slippery and utterly delicious. They turn up in soups of a robust nature and a few stir fries. Wheat noodles are sold dried (the *somen* often delightfully wrapped).

**Eggy ones (6)** These come both thick and thin, and are the typical, some might say archetypal Chinese noodles. They have a rich firm texture, not unlike egg pasta come to think of it. But we would not suggest that you substitute one for the other. Pasta for noodles that is. The process is different – of which more later. *Ramen* are classed as eggy noodles and have a defined place in Japanese cooking (see facing page). Available both fresh and dried.

# ingredients

**Chinese flowering chives**
Stronger than normal chives and flat rather than round-stemmed. Often referred to as garlic chives. Available in Asian stores. If substituting normal chives, double up on the quantity.

*Dashi*
A light fish stock made from *konbu* (see right) and dried bonito flakes.

*Dashi no moto*
An instant powdered version of *dashi*, commonly used in domestic kitchens in Japan.

**Enoki mushrooms**
Tight clusters of long-stemmed, creamy coloured mushrooms, enoki should retain a crunchy texture when cooked correctly. The flavour is delicate rather than full-bodied.

**Fermented black beans**
Salted black soy beans, traditionally used as a seasoning. You can buy them ready-prepared.

**Fish sauce (*nam pla*)**
A thin liquid extracted from salted, fermented fish. It deteriorates once opened and darkens with age. Fish sauce should be light golden brown with a tangy and salty flavour.

**Flowering greens (*choy sum*)**
A type of brassica related to pak choi and mustard greens. The flower looks pretty in cooked dishes.

**Galangal**
Galangal is from the same family as ginger but has a drier taste and is significantly more peppery and spicy. You can substitute one for the other, but be aware of their differences.

**Hoisin sauce**
Thick, dark and spicy, this soy-based sauce is easily obtainable.

**Kaffir lime leaves**
The leaf of a citrus tree. Dried or frozen ones are practically useless. Buy fresh and store in the fridge wrapped in cling film.

*Kamaboko-aka*
Japanese fishcakes, bought in rolls (see photograph on page 176), which are traditionally white with a pink outer crust. Available from Oriental stores.

*Katsuo bushi*
Dried fish flakes from the bonito fish (similar to tuna). You can add to salads or directly on to finished dishes but it is most commonly used to make *dashi* (see left).

*Kimchee*
Korean in origin, *kimchee* is pickled vegetables, most often Chinese cabbage, and fish. Most Koreans make their own, but you can buy commercial versions in Asian stores.

*Konbu*
Sold both dried and ready soaked, *konbu* is kelp seaweed. It delivers a fruity saltiness to dishes.

*Mirin*
Sake, which is combined with sugar so it has a sweet, tangy flavour. It's used in small quantities to give a smooth roundness to dishes.

*Miso*
*Miso* varies enormously from one brand to another. Essentially a paste made from fermented soya beans and combined with other ingredients. General all-purpose *miso*, made with brown rice, has a big, rich flavour while sweet white *miso* is much lighter and more delicate. It is best to experiment until you find one you like.

**Oyster sauce**
Thick, dark and brown, this meaty-flavoured sauce is made from a concentrate of oysters cooked with soy sauce. It is used both in cooking and as a condiment. For vegetarians there is an alternative made with mushrooms. Widely available.

**Rice vinegar**
Usually a light bronze colour, rice vinegar typically tastes sweet and mildly sour rather than sharp.

**Sake**
See page 187.

*Shichimi* or seven-spice pepper
A hot kick of chilli and black pepper combined with sesame, hemp and poppy seeds as well as orange peel and *nori* seaweed. Widely available in Asian stores this seasoning gives an extra kick, particularly to *soba* and *udon* dishes.

**Shiitake mushrooms**
Available in both a fresh and dried form. When fresh the flavour is quite muted with a pleasant crunchy texture. When dried, the flavour is much more concentrated and meaty and the texture is more firm. If dried they generally need to be soaked in hot water for 15–20 minutes.

**Soy sauce**
Light soy sauce is generally best for cooking and is suitable for most of the recipes in this book. Dark soy sauce gives a stronger colour and flavour and can also be used as a condiment.

**Thai basil**
Purple-stemmed but with green leaves. Thai basil has a strong aniseed flavour, which both sweetens dishes and adds a welcome aroma. Available from Asian stores.

**Tofu or bean curd**
Made from soya beans, tofu is rich in protein. There are essentially two kinds, firm and silken. The former is the one to use if any cooking is involved, the latter if it is being dressed and used in a salad or similar style of dish.

**Yellow bean sauce**
A mixture of yellow beans and salt, thickened with flour. It comes in two versions, whole beans and crushed or broken beans. The latter tends to be saltier. Available in Asian stores.

# stocks and preparations

It is impossible to over-emphasise the importance of good stock. It is a yardstick against which chefs are measured. In Japan, for example, a miso soup is a defining dish. A stock has to work on many levels, to satisfy so many criteria. It has to be well seasoned, but not too much. It has to be sweet, but not cloying. It has to have body, but only when it is in balance with everything else.

All this requires time, a commodity most of us severely lack. At wagamama we get round the issue by making stock in large batches to our own specification. This is not really possible at home, though, hence the recipes that follow.

Taking shortcuts is not something we entertain. But then we are not looking to try to put food on the table in the same way as you are. We may deliver dishes in minutes, but hours of work beforehand go into making that possible. What is important about the quicker versions of these stocks is that you realise what you are going to get. Something less, certainly, but also an experience that is tailored to the circumstances at the time.

There is nothing wrong with stock cubes. But not all cubes are the same. Some taste decidely better than others. And there are other useful stock products out there. Fresh stock sold in tubs for example, or powdered granules. What makes one good, or better, than another? Only you can decide.

As you work your way through this book you will find the recipes involve preparation which is then followed by the cooking. At first this may seem an odd way of working, frustrating even, as little seems to be happening. In practice, however, this route is tried and tested.

# other bits and pieces

How you chop is very important. Avoid right angles; they are difficult on the eye. And in the mouth. Diagonal slices are pleasing to look at and expose a greater surface area to heat and to other flavouring ingredients. Generally a good thing.

A wok is useful. But not essential. A frying pan will also work. There is no need to rush out and buy the kit. A fork, after all, will do the job of chopsticks. Only differently.

Stir frying is different from frying. You cook over a high heat. And quickly. Moving everything around. Either by tossing or using a scoop. Don't fall shy of this technique. It is key.

These dishes have generally been specified for two people on the basis a meal will be made up of two or three dishes. You might, or course, choose to double up one recipe for four. There are no hard and fast rules. It depends rather on what you like.

chicken stock (1) *when you're not in a hurry*

**1kg chicken bones • 350g pork bones • 1 onion, peeled and chopped 2 carrots (50g), chopped • 4 leeks (350g), sliced • 25g ginger root, sliced • 4 Chinese cabbage leaves, roughly chopped**

Put the meat bones in a large pan, cover with cold water and bring almost to the boil. Turn the heat right down and simmer for 2 hours, skimming off any froth that rises to the surface.

Add the vegetables and another 1 litre of water, bring almost to the boil again, lower the heat and simmer for a further hour. Remove from the heat and allow to cool. Strain off the liquid, return to the saucepan and simmer for 1 hour to reduce further. Season with the chicken stock seasoning below.

chicken stock seasoning

**2 teaspoons salt • 2 teaspoons sugar • small pinch of white pepper 1 teaspoon *dashi no moto* (see page 11)**

chicken stock (2) *when you need to make stock at the same time as cooking*

**2 good-quality chicken stock cubes • 500g uncooked chicken thighs or wings • 1 leek, finely chopped • 1 carrot, finely chopped • 1 litre water**

Combine all the solid ingredients in a pan, add the water and bring almost to boiling point, lower the heat and simmer for 30 minutes. Strain and proceed.

chicken stock (3) *when you want something to eat now!*

**2 good-quality chicken stock cubes • 1 leek, finely chopped • 1 carrot, roughly chopped • 2.5cm piece of ginger root, roughly chopped • 1 litre water**

Combine all the solid ingredients in a pan, cover with the water, bring to the boil, strain and proceed.

vegetable stock (1) *when you're not in a hurry*

**4 Chinese cabbage leaves • 450g potatoes, peeled • 1 small sweet potato • 2 carrots • 2 tablespoons chopped tinned tomatoes • ½ small butternut squash • 1 white onion • 1 red onion • 1 leek • 3 litres water**

Roughly chop all the vegetables and put in a large pan with the water. Bring to the boil, then lower the heat to a gentle simmer and cook, uncovered, for 3 hours. Turn off the heat, allow to cool and strain. Season with the vegetable seasoning below.

vegetable stock seasoning

**2 teaspoons salt • 2 teaspoons sugar • pinch of white pepper**

vegetable stock (2) *when you need to make stock at the same time as cooking*

**2 good-quality vegetable stock cubes • 2 Chinese cabbage leaves 2 carrots, roughly chopped • few sprigs of flat-leaf parsley • 3 litres water**

Place all the ingredients in a large pan and bring to the boil, lower the heat and simmer for 10–15 minutes if time, then strain.

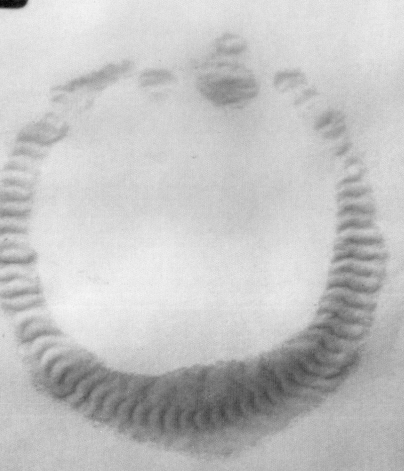

**wagamama** ★

# sauces

You can dip, dress, marinate, soak or season with a sauce. You can use a lot or a little, it's all up to you. Which we rather like. A sauce can come out of a container, and some of the best do. But making your own is not only enjoyable, it also gives you control. Soy sauce may be one to buy. Barbecue sauce on the other hand tends to be rather better when fashioned in your own kitchen.

The same is true of a green or red curry paste. Fresh ingredients pounded together tend to sing in a way that those in a container do not. It is something about the care, love and attention. There is likely to be more of that in your kitchen than a factory. At least, that's what we've found.

All these sauces are good keepers. Fridge friendly, they will happily sit things out for a while and then add zest and spice to a dish on demand. Maybe a dish that calls for them directly, or another one that does not. You never quite know how useful a good sauce can be. A dipping sauce, for example, does not always need to be dipped into. A splash or two over a bowl of *ramen* noodles can make for interesting eating.

You'll find other sauces in this book linked to specific dishes. In general these are more tailored to individual recipes but this doesn't mean they can't be used elsewhere. After all, if you like a sauce, it seems a shame not to eat it.

# sweet chilli dipping sauce

**makes about 200ml**

250g red chillies, trimmed
3 garlic cloves, peeled and roughly
    chopped
100g light brown sugar
2 teaspoons white wine vinegar

Combine everything in a small pan with 100ml water, bring to the boil and simmer over a moderate heat until soft, about 5 minutes. Blitz in a blender and season with a scant teaspoon of salt. Return to the pan, simmer for a further 10 minutes, taking care not to let it catch on the bottom. Allow to cool and refrigerate.

*Many bought sweet chilli sauces deliver too much sweetness and not a lot of character in the chilli, two things which you maintain control over when you make this all-purpose sauce at home. It will last indefinitely in the fridge and is, according to some, rather good on a bacon sandwich in place of ketchup.*

# red curry paste

**makes enough for 2–3 recipes**

10 dried red chillies, soaked in
    hot water and roughly chopped
3cm piece of ginger or galangal
    root, peeled and finely chopped
2 lemongrass stalks, outer leaves
    removed, finely chopped
zest of 2 limes
1 tablespoon finely chopped
    coriander stems
1 tablespoon chopped shallots
1 tablespoon chopped garlic
1 teaspoon light brown sugar
salt and white pepper
vegetable oil

Pound each ingredient, adding them one after the other, in a pestle and mortar. Season with salt and pepper and stir in enough oil to form a paste.

*You can always buy curry pastes (red and green) but none will be as fresh-tasting and invigorating as making your own. This will last for a few weeks in the fridge covered with a slick of vegetable oil.*

# yasai soba dressing

**makes about 250ml**

200ml teriyaki sauce, home
    made (see page 19) or bought
75ml yellow bean sauce
1 lemongrass stalk, outer leaves
    removed, finely sliced
1 tablespoon peeled and grated
    fresh ginger root

Put all the ingredients in a mixing bowl and combine until blended.

*You can dress noodles with this sauce, or put a blob on the side or top of a dish. You can dip a gyoza in it, or add a little to a salad dressing. It's very Asian in taste and attitude. It will keep for months in the fridge.*

# green curry paste

**makes about 150g**

6 green chillies, roughly chopped
1 lemongrass stalk, outer leaves
    removed, thinly sliced
3 kaffir lime leaves, finely sliced
1cm piece of ginger root, peeled
    and grated
bunch of coriander, stems finely
    chopped (leaves reserved for
    another dish)
1 teaspoon cumin seeds, roasted
    in a hot, dry frying pan
2 garlic cloves, peeled and roughly
    chopped
1 tablespoon finely chopped shallot
1 teaspoon shrimp paste
    (available from Oriental stores)
1 tablespoon vegetable oil

Blitz all the ingredients in a processor or pound in a pestle and mortar to a fine paste.

*As with the red version (see page 16) making this at home ensures a vibrant lively paste which will make no end of difference to your finished dish. You can buy green curry paste, but it rarely makes the grade. At least we don't think so. This will keep indefinitely in the fridge.*

# chilli ramen sauce

**makes about 125ml**

2 scant teaspoons sugar
2 tablespoons malt vinegar
3 tablespoons bought sweet
    chilli sauce
5 tablespoons fish sauce (*nam pla*)

Dissolve the sugar in the vinegar in a small pan over a gentle heat, allow to cool and then combine with the other ingredients.

*Using sugar as a seasoning is widely practised in Asia and this sauce is no exception. It brings a real meatiness to dishes and is generally lightly drizzled over food. It will keep for several weeks in the fridge.*

# teriyaki sauce

makes about 125ml

110g sugar
4 tablespoons light soy sauce
2 tablespoons sake
1 teaspoon dark soy sauce

Place the sugar and light soy sauce in a small pan over a low heat and stir until the sugar has dissolved. Simmer for 5 minutes until thick, add the sake and dark soy sauce and allow to cool.

*This sauce is most commonly used to brush meat with so it can marinate before it is grilled. You can also use it as a dipping sauce or to drizzle over noodles in broth. It will keep for a few weeks in the fridge.*

# barbecue sauce

makes about 200ml

100ml bought yellow bean sauce
100ml bought hoisin sauce
2 teaspoons sugar
2 garlic cloves, peeled and finely
    minced
1 tablespoon toasted sesame oil
pinch of white pepper
1 tablespoon dark soy sauce
2 tablespoons light soy sauce

Combine all the ingredients together in a small bowl.

*There are lots of brands of barbecue sauce, each one with its advocates. Making your own allows for variation (alter the amounts of each ingredient used) but most importantly makes you realise how bright and vibrant this sauce can be. Keeps in the fridge for several days.*

# kare lomen sauce

makes about 125ml

2 lemongrass stalks, outer leaves
    removed, roughly chopped
2.5cm piece of galangal root,
    peeled and roughly chopped
2 garlic cloves, peeled and finely
    chopped
2 onions, peeled and roughly chopped
1 red pepper, deseeded and
    roughly chopped
1 teaspoon sweet paprika
1 teaspoon fennel seeds
½ teaspoon chilli powder
½ teaspoon turmeric
½ teaspoon curry powder
1 teaspoon shrimp paste
    (available from Oriental stores)

**Combine all the ingredients in a blender and blitz to a smooth consistency.**

*This is a bright and invigorating sauce (see picture on left). It has a Thai theme with all that lemongrass and galangal. It will keep for a few days in the fridge.*

# tori kara age sauce

makes about 750ml

2.5cm piece of ginger root, peeled
    and grated
750ml light soy sauce
50ml sake
1 teaspoon sugar
1 tablespoon oyster sauce

**Combine all the ingredients in a pan and heat gently to dissolve the sugar. Set aside to cool.**

*Ginger and soy, soy and ginger. The combination is a winning one whichever way you say it. This is a marinade, a dipping sauce and something to drizzle over pretty much anything, from grilled fish and meat, to noodles sitting in a scant broth with or without other things. Keeps for several weeks in the fridge.*

# chilli sauce

makes about 300ml

2 tablespoons vegetable oil

2 lemongrass stalks, outer leaves
    removed, finely chopped

1 teaspoon peeled and grated fresh
    ginger root

1 chilli, finely chopped

1 red onion, peeled and finely
    chopped

2 garlic cloves, peeled and finely
    chopped

½ teaspoon salt

½ teaspoon sugar

1 tablespoon light soy sauce

1 red pepper, deseeded and
    finely chopped

1 tablespoon bought sweet
    chilli sauce

1 tablespoon tomato ketchup

300ml water

Heat the vegetable oil in a small pan over a low heat until hot. Add the next eight ingredients and sauté for 7–8 minutes without colouring. Add the red pepper and continue cooking gently for 8–10 minutes. Add the remaining ingredients, bring to the boil and simmer for 10 minutes. Blitz in a blender and use.

*There is a rounded fruitiness to this sauce allied to a hefty kick, which, if you choose, you can down-play simply by reducing the amount of chilli used. Generally used as a dipping sauce. It will keep for a few days in the fridge.*

# soy dipping sauce

makes 2 servings

2 tablespoons soy sauce

1 tablespoon water

½ teaspoon sugar

½ teaspoon peeled and grated
    fresh ginger root

2 shallots, finely chopped

dash of toasted sesame oil

Combine all the ingredients, stir to dissolve the sugar, and serve.

*Light, bright and full of interest, this sauce is for dipping certainly, but can also be used as a finishing sauce for other dishes. Keeps for several weeks in the fridge.*

# sweet miso dressing

makes about 125ml

2 tablespoons *mirin* (see page 11)
2 tablespoons sake
4 tablespoons sugar
110g *miso* paste (see page 11)
1 tablespoon chilli oil
1 tablespoon vegetable oil
2 teaspoons *shichimi* (see page 11)

Put the *mirin* and sake in a small pan and bring to the boil. Lower the heat, add the sugar and stir until dissolved. Pour onto the *miso* paste and beat until smooth. Add the oils and *shichimi* and mix thoroughly.

*Miso brings a deliciously meaty quality to dishes. Here it is used in a dressing, so it is designed to enhance dishes. But a dish of noodles dressed in this sauce makes for quite a nice snack. It will keep for several days in the fridge.*

# gyoza sauce

makes about 350ml

1 large garlic clove, peeled and
    finely chopped
1 large red chilli, finely chopped
salt
25g sugar
100ml malt vinegar
250ml light soy sauce
1 tablespoon toasted sesame oil

Mash the garlic and chilli together with a little salt with the side of your knife to form a paste. Dissolve the sugar in the vinegar in a small pan over a low heat. Combine everything and store in a sealed container.

*A great dipping sauce. It also adds interest to finished dishes and is good for dipping grilled fish and meat into. It will keep for several weeks in the fridge.*

# souped up

wagamama *ramen* is the sort of food wagamama was built on. Noodles and a delicious broth along with some select vegetables and meat. Easy to cook. Simple to serve. Delicious. And good for you.

We cannot claim to have invented this combination. It has existed in the East for centuries. Noodle stalls are an original fast food source. Maybe the original fast food. Simplicity at its best.

It is easy to soup things up. We do it all the time. But only once in a while do we come up with a real winner. A few of these appear in the following pages. What makes a soup win? It's something to do with satisfaction. A licking of the lips. A sigh of contentment.

Noodles have this effect. Particularly when the broth is good. You can cut corners with the broth. Some do. But we don't advise it. This is the one chapter when a really good stock will show off its best. This is not to forget the other ingredients. But don't skimp on the stock.

What is your soup about? If you don't know, how are your noodles expected to? There needs to be a plan. Which is why we are very careful when working on new soups. A wagamama *ramen* is quite hard to beat, or at least to equal. Which is sort of where our benchmark lies. A marker that makes us happy. Proud even.

A word about your bowls. We use ramen bowls, which are large, wide and made from melamine. This allows you to pick them up, the closer to slurp from without burning your hands. Any big bowl will suffice. It rather depends on how much slurping you wish to do.

serves 2

100g *somen* noodles
2 tablespoons vegetable oil
salt and white pepper
100g firm tofu, cut into 1cm cubes
1 red onion, peeled and finely
    sliced
1 small potato, peeled and
    thinly sliced
1 medium carrot, grated
1 red chilli, deseeded and finely
    sliced
1 green chilli, deseeded and
    finely sliced
250ml chicken stock (see
    page 13)
30g white *miso* paste (see page 11)
1 tablespoon soy sauce
1 sheet of *nori* seaweed
2 spring onions, white part only,
    sliced thinly (to serve)

# tofu and miso soup with somen noodles

Soften the noodles according to the instructions on the packet, drain and refresh under cold water.

Heat 1 tablespoon of the vegetable oil in a hot wok. Season the tofu and stir fry until golden on all sides, remove and drain on kitchen paper.

Heat the remaining oil in the wok, add the red onion and potato, and stir fry over a moderate heat for 2 minutes. Add the carrot, red and green chillies and cook for a further minute. Add 250ml water, the chicken stock, *miso* paste and reserved tofu. Season with soy sauce, salt and pepper.

Bring to the boil, reduce the heat and simmer for 5 minutes or until the potato is cooked.

Meanwhile cut the *nori* into strips. Heat in a dry frying pan over a moderate heat for a scant minute to crisp up.

Divide the noodles into 2 bowls, pour over the soup and serve topped with slices of *nori* and spring onions.

# tofu, lettuce and egg noodle soup

serves 2

100g egg noodles
4 tablespoons vegetable oil
salt and white pepper
100g tofu (smoked if possible),
    cut into 1cm cubes
1 carrot, julienned
2 spring onions, finely sliced
1 tablespoon finely sliced shallot
2 garlic cloves, peeled and finely
    sliced
500ml vegetable stock (see
    page 13)
1 teaspoon soy sauce
2 teaspoons fish sauce (*nam pla*)
scant teaspoon sugar
2 teaspoons *mirin* (see page 11)
1 head little gem lettuce, shredded

Cook the noodles according to the instructions on the packet, drain and refresh under cold water. Heat the wok on a high heat, add 2 tablespoons of the oil. Season the tofu and fry until golden brown on all sides. Remove and drain on kitchen paper.

Wipe out the wok and return to the heat. Add the remaining oil then stir fry the carrot, spring onions, shallot and garlic until the carrot is tender, about 2 minutes. Add the vegetable stock, soy sauce, fish sauce, sugar and *mirin* and bring to the boil. Add the lettuce, season with salt and pepper to taste.

Divide the noodles and tofu between 2 bowls, ladle over the hot soup and serve.

# three-mushroom soup

serves 2

2 dried shiitake mushrooms
75g *ramen* noodles
2 teaspoons vegetable oil
1 carrot, peeled and finely sliced
2 teaspoons finely sliced shallots
50g enoki mushrooms, broken up
25g button mushrooms, sliced
handful of baby spinach
handful of mangetout, thinly sliced
300ml chicken stock (see
    page 13)
1 sheet of *konbu* (kelp) seaweed
2 teaspoons soy sauce
½ teaspoon sugar
2 teaspoons rice vinegar
1 teaspoon *miso* paste (see
    page 11)
scant 2 teaspoons sesame seeds,
    briefly toasted in a hot, dry
    frying pan

Pour 150ml boiling water over the mushrooms and set aside to soak.

Cook the noodles according to the instructions on the packet, drain and refresh under cold water.

Heat the oil in a hot wok and stir fry the carrot and shallots for 5 minutes. Drain the shiitake (reserving the liquid), and discard any tough stalks. Slice thinly and add them to the wok with the other mushrooms, spinach and mangetout. Continue to stir fry for a further 3 minutes.

Bring the stock to the boil, adding the liquid from the mushrooms. Add the *konbu*, soy sauce, sugar, rice vinegar, *miso* and noodles to the wok, toss well so that everything is combined. Pour in the boiling stock and bring to the boil.

Divide between 2 bowls, and serve scattered with the toasted sesame seeds.

200g flat egg noodles

1 tablespoon vegetable oil

1 carrot, peeled and julienned

2 lemongrass stalks, outer leaves
    removed, finely chopped

1 chilli, finely sliced

2 garlic cloves, peeled and sliced

2 kaffir lime leaves

200g skate

250ml chicken stock (see
    page 13)

2 tablespoons rice vinegar

100g raw, peeled prawns

4 scallops, sliced horizontally

2 handfuls of spinach

1 head little gem lettuce, shredded

salt and white pepper

pickled ginger

# spring greens and seafood soup with pickled ginger

Cook the noodles according to the instructions on the packet, drain and refresh under cold water.

Heat the oil in a hot wok and stir fry the carrot, lemongrass, chilli, garlic and kaffir lime leaves for 1 minute. Add the skate, chicken stock and rice vinegar and reduce the heat. Poach the skate for 5 minutes, turning halfway through until it just comes away from the bone. Remove and set aside to cool. As soon as you can handle it, slide the meat off the bones.

Add the prawns, scallops, spinach and lettuce to the hot stock. Season with salt and pepper. Cook over a low heat for 3–4 minutes or until the scallops and prawns are cooked through and the leaves wilted. Add the noodles and skate to the pan and toss so that everything is well combined and heated through.

Ladle into 4 bowls and serve topped with pickled ginger.

serves 4

1 tablespoon vegetable oil

1 red onion, peeled and thinly sliced

2 garlic cloves, peeled and minced

2 lemongrass stalks, outer leaves
    removed, finely sliced

100g button mushrooms, thinly
    sliced

½ teaspoon sugar

2 teaspoons fish sauce (*nam pla*)

1 litre chicken stock (see page 13)

8 scallops

8 raw, unpeeled prawns

16 mussels, in the shell

zest and juice of 1 lime

100g medium egg noodles

1 red chilli, sliced

2 teaspoons toasted sesame oil

3 spring onions, thinly sliced

# seafood and egg noodle soup

Heat the vegetable oil in a hot wok and stir fry the onion, garlic, lemongrass and mushrooms for 1 minute. Add the sugar, fish sauce and chicken stock. Bring to the boil.

Add the seafood. Bring to the boil. Add the lime zest and juice, the noodles and the chilli. Simmer until the noodles are tender and the seafood cooked, about 3 minutes.

Divide between 4 bowls, drizzle over the sesame oil and scatter over the spring onions.

# hot and sour seafood broth

serves 2

150g raw tiger prawns, peeled
    and deveined, shells reserved
1 litre vegetable stock (see
    page 13)
1 green chilli, deseeded and finely
    sliced
½ teaspoon salt
6 kaffir lime leaves
2 lemongrass stalks, smashed
100g rice noodles
1 small squid, cut into rings
1 tablespoon fish sauce (*nam pla*)
juice of 1 lime
6 shiitake mushrooms, stems
    removed, thinly sliced
2 spring onions, thinly sliced
6 cooked crab claws, cracked
2 tablespoons roughly chopped
    coriander

Combine the prawn shells, stock, chilli, salt, lime leaves and lemongrass in a pan and bring to the boil, reduce the heat, cover and simmer for 30 minutes. Strain into a clean pan.

Cook the noodles according to the instructions on the packet, drain and refresh under cold water.

Mix together the prawns, squid, fish sauce, lime juice, mushrooms and spring onions. Season with salt and toss gently.

Bring the strained liquor back to the boil. Add the prawn and squid mixture along with the crab claws and simmer for 2 minutes. Taste and correct seasoning if required.

Place the soaked noodles in 2 bowls and ladle over the hot broth. Serve scattered with the coriander leaves.

# prawn and quail's egg soup

serves 2

6 raw, unpeeled prawns
500ml chicken stock (see
    page 13)
2 teaspoons *mirin* (see page 11)
1 tablespoon soy sauce
2 teaspoons sake
3cm piece of ginger root, peeled
    and julienned
1 garlic clove, peeled and finely
    sliced
100g rice vermicelli
handful of mangetout
2 pak choi, separated into leaves
4 quail's eggs
2 spring onions, finely sliced
large handful of coriander leaves

Remove the shells (and heads if available) from the prawns, devein and set the prawns aside. Combine the shells (and heads) with the stock, *mirin,* soy sauce, sake, ginger and garlic in a pan and bring to the boil. Simmer for 10 minutes then remove the prawn shells.

Soak the vermicelli according to the instructions on the packet, drain and refresh under cold water.

Cook the mangetout and pak choi in the stock for 5 minutes or until cooked. Add the prawns, simmer for a scant 2 minutes and remove from the heat.

Divide the vermicelli between 2 bowls and add the prawns and vegetables. Poach the quail's eggs in the remaining broth over a medium heat for 2 minutes and spoon them over the other ingredients, along with the stock. Check the seasoning and serve scattered with the spring onions and coriander.

# hot and sour seafood ramen

**for the marinade**

2 teaspoons fish sauce (*nam pla*)

2 teaspoons *mirin* (see page 11)

2 teaspoons soy sauce

dash of Tabasco

2 teaspoons cornflour

350g raw, unpeeled, mixed seafood
     (prawns, scallops, clams,
     mussels)

salt and white pepper

75g *ramen* noodles

350ml chicken stock (see
     page 13)

1 stick cinnamon

3 cloves

1 tablespoon rice vinegar

1 teaspoon sugar

1 red chilli (or to taste), finely sliced

2 teaspoons fish sauce (*nam pla*)

50g baby corn, halved lengthways

50g courgettes, thinly sliced

6 pieces of pickled bamboo
     shoots (*menma*)

5g *wakame* seaweed, soaked in
     warm water for 5 minutes and
     roughly sliced

4 spring onions, finely sliced

few sprigs of watercress

To make the marinade, whisk the fish sauce, *mirin*, soy sauce and Tabasco into the cornflour. Season the seafood with salt and pepper and add to the marinade, coating well. Set aside for an hour; overnight in the fridge is even better.

Cook the noodles according to the instructions on the packet, drain and refresh under cold water.

Bring the chicken stock, cinnamon, cloves, rice vinegar, sugar, chilli and fish sauce to the boil and add the seafood, marinade, baby corn and courgettes. Simmer for 3 minutes, or until the seafood is cooked.

Divide the noodles between 2 bowls, top with the seafood and vegetables and ladle in the stock. Check the seasoning and serve topped with the bamboo shoots, *wakame*, spring onions and watercress.

100g *ramen* noodles

1 small egg

60g plain flour

vegetable oil, for frying

2 garlic cloves, peeled and chopped

1 leek, trimmed and sliced

50g mangetout

1 carrot, peeled and thinly
    sliced on the diagonal

1 onion, peeled and sliced

2 teaspoons soy sauce

1 tablespoon rice vinegar

1 tablespoon fish sauce (*nam pla*)

2 star anise

500ml chicken stock (see page 13)

10 raw, peeled tiger prawns

2 teaspoons toasted sesame oil

bought sweet chilli sauce

# crispy prawn ramen soup

Cook the noodles according to the instructions on the packet, drain and refresh under cold water.

Lightly whisk the egg in a bowl with 100ml iced water. Sieve in the flour and barely combine to make a smooth batter (don't overwork it, or it will become heavy).

Heat 1 tablespoon of oil in a hot wok and stir fry the garlic, leek, mangetout, carrot, onion, soy sauce, rice vinegar, fish sauce and star anise for 2 minutes. Pour in the chicken stock, bring to the boil and simmer for 5 minutes.

Heat 3cm of vegetable oil to 180°C in a wok or deep-sided pan. Drop in a little batter to test the temperature; if it bubbles up and turns golden, you are ready to go. Dip each prawn in the batter (you won't require all of it) and fry for 30 seconds to 1 minute or until crisp and golden. Remove and drain on kitchen paper.

Ladle the soup and noodles into 2 bowls, ensuring there is an island of noodles surrounded by broth. Drizzle with the sesame oil and top with the prawns. Serve with the chilli sauce.

serves 2

150g firm tofu

vegetable oil, for frying

250g *ramen* noodles

4 slices *kamaboko-aka* (see
    page 11)

4 crabsticks

1 egg, hard-boiled

4 cooked and peeled prawns

2 pak choi, roughly chopped

1 litre chicken stock (see page 13)

2 boneless, skinless chicken breasts

salt and white pepper

12 pieces of pickled bamboo
    shoots (*menma*), drained

1 tablespoon *wakame* seaweed,
    soaked in warm water for
    5 minutes, drained and chopped

2 spring onions, sliced

# wagamama ramen

Cut the tofu into 1cm slices and pan fry in a little oil for about 1 minute on each side until just coloured.

Cook the noodles according to the instructions on the packet, drain and refresh under cold running water. Divide between 2 bowls along with the *kamaboko-aka,* crabsticks, tofu, half an egg each, 2 prawns each and the pak choi.

Bring the chicken stock to the boil. Preheat the grill or a griddle. Lightly coat the chicken breasts in vegetable oil, season with salt and pepper and grill or chargrill for 4 minutes each side or until cooked. Allow to rest for 5 minutes and slice on the diagonal into 1cm strips.

To serve, pour the chicken stock over the noodles, lay the chicken strips on top and garnish with the *menma, wakame* and spring onions.

*If we have a signature dish then this is it; pure wagamama. Broth, noodles and a host of toppings so lots of variety. This is the only recipe you'll also find in* The wagamama Cookbook. *We are rather proud of it.*

# crab and wonton broth

serves 4

1 medium, cooked crab

vegetable oil

salt and white pepper

1 carrot, roughly chopped

1 celery stick, roughly chopped

1 onion, roughly chopped

500ml chicken stock (see
    page 13)

100g rice vermicelli

2 eggs, 1 separated, 1 lightly
    beaten

1cm piece of ginger root,
    peeled and minced

2 teaspoons finely chopped
    spring onion

1 garlic clove, peeled and minced

small bunch of coriander, leaves
    picked, stems finely chopped

8 wonton wrappers

2 small pak choi, trimmed
    and separated

handful of mangetout

100g carrots, peeled and cut into
    5mm dice

100g celeriac, peeled and cut into
    5mm dice

2 teaspoons soy sauce

Preheat the oven to 200°C/gas mark 6. Crack the crab shell with the back of a large knife. Pick the crabmeat, keeping the white and brown meat separate. Discard the 'dead man's fingers'.

Place the crab shells in a roasting tin, toss with a little vegetable oil, season well with salt and roast for 20 minutes. Transfer to a saucepan, add the carrot, celery and onion and pour over the chicken stock. Bring to the boil slowly, skim and simmer for 30 minutes, skimming the surface as necessary. Stir in the egg white, simmer for 5 minutes then turn off the heat.

Line a sieve with a double layer of muslin, pour the stock through and leave to drain into a clean saucepan. (This may sound like quite a performance but it means you will have a clear stock in the finished dish which looks and tastes very impressive.)

Combine the brown crabmeat with the egg yolk, ginger, spring onion, garlic and the chopped coriander stems. Season with salt and pepper to taste.

Place a teaspoon of this crab mixture in the centre of 4 of the wonton wrappers, dab the edges with the beaten egg, cover with a second skin and seal, pushing out as much air as you can. Poach the wontons in boiling salted water for 5 minutes, drain, refresh under cold water and set aside. Blanch the pak choi and mangetout in the same water for about 15 seconds, drain and refresh under cold water.

Cook the vermicelli according to the instructions on the packet, drain and refresh under cold water.

Now blanch the carrots and celeriac in boiling salted water for 1 minute, refresh under cold water and transfer to 2 bowls. Add the wontons and vermicelli and cover with the clear broth. Add the pak choi and mangetout and sprinkle with the white crabmeat. Season with the soy sauce and serve.

# marinated salmon ramen

serves 2

**for the marinade**

3cm piece of ginger root,
  peeled and grated
2 teaspoons *mirin* (see page 11)
2 teaspoons soy sauce
2 teaspoons fish sauce (*nam pla*)

2 salmon pieces
  (approximately 150g each)
salt and white pepper
100g *ramen* noodles
500ml chicken stock (see
  page 13)
2 teaspoons fish sauce (*nam pla*)
2 garlic cloves, peeled and minced
1 carrot, peeled and julienned
½ cucumber, deseeded
  and julienned
50g French beans, trimmed
  and halved lengthways
handful of coriander leaves

Combine the marinade ingredients in a bowl. Season the salmon pieces with salt and pepper and add to the marinade. Turn to coat several times and set aside for 1 hour; overnight in the fridge is even better.

Cook the noodles according to the instructions on the packet, drain and refresh under cold water.

Combine the chicken stock with the fish sauce and garlic and bring to the boil. Add the salmon and its marinade, cover and simmer for 2–3 minutes. Add the carrot, cucumber and French beans and simmer for a further 2–3 minutes or until the fish is just cooked. Remove the fish and keep warm.

Divide the noodles between 2 bowls. Pour over the soup, ensuring each bowl gets an equal share of vegetables. Check the seasoning. Top with the fish and serve scattered with coriander leaves.

# vietnamese-style crab noodle soup

serves 2

200g rice vermicelli
1 tablespoon fish sauce (*nam pla*)
1 teaspoon sugar
salt and white pepper
1 litre chicken stock (see page 13)
150g flaked white crabmeat
1 head little gem lettuce, finely
  shredded
2 teaspoons finely sliced spring
  onion
50g beansprouts
1 lime, cut into wedges

Cook the vermicelli according to the instructions on the packet, drain and refresh under cold water.

Combine the fish sauce, sugar and a generous pinch of salt in a saucepan with the stock, bring to the boil, lower the heat and simmer gently for 20 minutes.

Add the crabmeat, check and adjust the seasoning if necessary and remove from the heat.

Divide the noodles between 2 bowls. Ladle the soup over the noodles, top with the lettuce, spring onion and beansprouts and serve with the lime wedges.

# marinated sea bass with green vegetables and ramen noodles

for the marinade

2 teaspoons soy sauce

1 tablespoon toasted sesame oil

2 teaspoons fish sauce (*nam pla*)

2 teaspoons *mirin* (see page 11)

2 teaspoons cornflour

200g sea bass fillets (skin on),
    cut into 3cm pieces

salt and white pepper

100g *ramen* noodles

1 litre chicken stock (see page 13)

2 garlic cloves, peeled and minced

3cm piece of ginger root, peeled
    and grated

1 tablespoon fish sauce (*nam pla*)

1 tablespoon rice vinegar

juice of 1 lime

handful of French beans, trimmed

2 tablespoons frozen peas,
    defrosted

handful of spinach

handful of coriander leaves

To make the marinade, combine the soy sauce, sesame oil, fish sauce and *mirin*. Stir in the cornflour to dissolve. Combine the fish with the marinade ingredients, season with salt and pepper and set aside for an hour; overnight in the fridge is even better.

Cook the noodles according to the instructions on the packet, drain and refresh under cold water.

Combine the chicken stock, garlic, ginger, fish sauce, rice vinegar and lime juice in a pan and bring to the boil. Blanch the beans in this mixture for 4–5 minutes, until just tender. Remove with a sieve or tongs and refresh under cold water.

Add the fish pieces and marinade to the simmering stock, bring to the boil for 2 minutes then add the beans, the peas and spinach to the pan with the noodles and simmer for a further minute. Check the seasoning.

Divide between 4 bowls and serve scattered with coriander leaves.

# chargrilled chicken, soba and miso soup

serves 2

for the marinade

2 teaspoons hoisin sauce

1 teaspoon fish sauce (*nam pla*)

1 teaspoon *mirin* (see page 11)

1 chicken breast

750ml chicken stock (see page 13)

1 tablespoon red *miso* paste (see
    page 11)

3cm piece of ginger root,
    peeled and thinly sliced

2 garlic cloves, peeled and sliced

200g *soba* noodles

2 pak choi, roughly chopped

1 hard-boiled egg, shelled
    and halved

To make the marinade, combine the hoisin sauce, fish sauce and *mirin*. Add the chicken breast and toss well. Set aside for an hour; overnight in the fridge is even better.

Chargrill or grill the chicken for 4–5 minutes each side until cooked.

Place the chicken stock, *miso* paste, ginger and garlic in a pan and bring to the boil. Add the *soba* noodles and pak choi and cook for 3 minutes or until the noodles are just cooked.

Divide the soup between 2 bowls, ensuring each has an equal share of noodles. Slice the chicken on the diagonal and place on the noodles and broth. Top with half a hard-boiled egg and serve.

# hot and sour chicken ramen

serves 2

for the marinade

2 teaspoons *mirin* (see page 11)

1 tablespoon fish sauce (*nam pla*)

1 red chilli, thinly sliced

1 garlic clove, peeled and minced

150g dark chicken meat (leg
    and thigh), trimmed and
    roughly chopped

salt and black pepper

750ml chicken stock (see
    page 13)

2 star anise

1 stick cinnamon

1 tablespoon rice vinegar

1 teaspoon honey

2 heads pak choi, sliced

75g *ramen* noodles

few sprigs of coriander

To make the marinade, mix the ingredients in a medium bowl. Add the chicken, season with salt and black pepper and toss so that everything is well combined. Cover and leave for 1 hour; overnight in the fridge is even better.

Heat the chicken stock along with the star anise, cinnamon, rice vinegar and honey. When boiling add the chicken and its marinade, pak choi and the noodles. Bring back to the boil and simmer for 3–4 minutes or until the chicken is cooked. Remove any scum from the surface of the water.

Divide between 2 bowls and serve topped with the coriander.

# chilli pork ramen

serves 2

2 entrecote pork steaks
2 tablespoons barbecue sauce
    (see page 19)
100g thin *soba* noodles
500ml chicken stock (see
    page 13)
1 tablespoon chilli *ramen* sauce
    (see page 18)
bunch of coriander, leaves picked
large handful of beansprouts
1 small red onion, peeled
    and thinly sliced
1 red chilli, deseeded and
    thinly sliced
1 lime, cut into wedges
teriyaki sauce (see page 19)

Combine the pork with the barbecue sauce in a plastic bag, massage and set aside for 1 hour; overnight in the fridge is even better.

Grill the pork on both sides for 3–4 minutes or until cooked. Allow to rest and then slice on the diagonal.

Cook the noodles according to the instructions on the packet, drain and refresh under cold water.

Heat the chicken stock. Combine the noodles, chilli *ramen* sauce, coriander leaves, beansprouts, onion and chilli and divide between 2 bowls. Ladle over the hot stock, top with the sliced pork and serve with a lime wedge and the teriyaki dipping sauce.

*This recipe is by Sjoerd Hoek, from wagamama in Amsterdam.*

# pork, prawn and egg noodle soup

serves 2

100g medium egg noodles
2 tablespoons vegetable oil
2 garlic cloves, peeled and
    thinly sliced
50g minced pork
25g raw, peeled prawns
750ml chicken stock (see
    page 13)
1 tablespoon fish sauce (*nam pla*)
2 Chinese cabbage, stem removed
    and leaves cut into rough strips
2 teaspoons toasted sesame oil
2 spring onions, thinly sliced
50g beansprouts
1 tablespoon coriander leaves
1 tablespoon roasted peanuts
1 lime, cut into wedges

Cook the noodles according to the instructions on the packet, drain and refresh under cold water.

Heat a small frying pan over a medium heat, add 1 tablespoon of oil and fry the garlic for 1 minute until crisp and golden. Toss the garlic and the hot oil through the noodles and reserve.

Heat a heavy-bottomed pan over a medium heat, add the remaining oil and cook the minced pork until it begins to brown, about 5 minutes.

Add the prawns, the stock and fish sauce and bring to the boil. Add the cabbage and simmer for 30 seconds, check and correct the seasoning if necessary and remove from the heat.

Divide the garlic noodles between bowls, ladle over the soup and add the sesame oil. Top with the spring onions, beansprouts and coriander leaves. Sprinkle with chopped peanuts and serve with the lime wedges.

# clear beef noodle soup with tashima

serves 2

2 sheets *tashima* (dried kelp) seaweed
100g *udon* noodles
100g beef sirloin
500ml chicken stock (see page 13)
salt and white pepper
1 teaspoon soy sauce
1 spring onion, sliced
1 garlic clove, peeled and crushed

Cut several thin strips of seaweed and reserve. Soak the rest in warm water for 30 minutes. Drain, rinse carefully and cut into 5cm lengths.

Cook the noodles according to the instructions on the packet, drain and refresh under cold water.

Cut the beef into bite-sized pieces. Bring the stock to the boil. Season the beef with salt and pepper and add to the stock, stirring to ensure the meat isn't stuck together. Add the soy sauce, spring onion and garlic and skim off any impurities. Reduce the heat and simmer for 10 minutes. Add the noodles and simmer for a further 5 minutes. Add the soaked seaweed and check the seasoning.

Divide between 2 bowls, top with the reserved seaweed strips, and serve immediately.

# rich beef noodle soup

serves 2

for the stock
600g beef bones
400g pork bones
2 star anise
1 stick cinnamon
3cm piece of ginger root, peeled and sliced
1 onion, quartered

100g *udon* noodles
2 tablespoons vegetable oil
2 garlic cloves, peeled and finely sliced
1 tablespoon finely sliced shallots
200g rump steak, trimmed and very thinly sliced
2 tablespoons soy sauce
2 tablespoons fish sauce (*nam pla*)
salt and white pepper
handful of beansprouts
large handful of coriander leaves
large handful of mint leaves

Combine all the stock ingredients in a pan, cover with 2.5 litres cold water and bring to the boil. Periodically skim off the scum that will form on the surface to stop the broth going cloudy. Simmer for 2 hours. Strain into a clean saucepan, bring back to the boil and reduce by half, for about 30 minutes. You should have about 650ml of rich stock.

Cook the noodles according to the instructions on the packet, drain and refresh under cold water.

Heat the oil in a hot wok and sauté the garlic until golden; remove and set aside. Add the shallots and stir fry until golden and crisp, remove and add to the garlic.

Divide the noodles between 2 bowls. Add the beef, soy sauce and fish sauce to the broth and simmer for 2 minutes or until the beef is just cooked. Check the seasoning.

Ladle the beef and stock over the noodles. Serve topped with the beansprouts, coriander, mint and crispy garlic and shallots.

*Simmering the stock for 2 hours may sound like a stage you might want to skip, but it is the essence of this dish.*

Wa

# wrapped

You normally dress a noodle. Or soak it in a broth. But there is a way that turns this notion on its head. Wrapping noodles do that. Round or square, they envelop a neat pile of deliciousness. This might be vegetables. Usually there is protein too. Typically minced, or cut small. With some you dip. With others all the punch is contained within. In others still the noodle not only wraps, but turns up in the filling too. Usually these are the slippery ones (see page 9).

Wrapped noodles make great finger food. Packaging you can and do want to eat. They work on picnics, shine at parties and generally encourage a pretty relaxed view about eating. If you steam or boil you end up with something soft – silky even. At least that's before you get to the filling, when things get really interesting.

If you fry or bake the result ends up being decidedly more crispy on the outside. When we choose this route we tend to go for strong robust flavours inside.

You can, of course, opt not to do any of these things and simply soak your wrapper and, well, wrap. Perfect if the stuffing is a salad or cooked ingredients.

30g dried Chinese mushrooms
50g rice vermicelli
1 garlic clove, peeled and finely
    chopped
1 tablespoon finely chopped
    spring onion
100g water chestnuts, finely
    chopped
1 tablespoon soy sauce
1 tablespoon *mirin* (see page 11)
1 tablespoon toasted sesame oil
1 red chilli, finely diced
1 tablespoon fish sauce (*nam pla*)
½ teaspoon light brown soft sugar
50g beansprouts
1 tablespoon roughly chopped mint
1 tablespoon roughly chopped
    coriander
100g Chinese cabbage, finely sliced
salt and white pepper
chilli sauce (see page 22)

20cm or 16cm rice paper wrappers

# pancake rolls

Soak the mushrooms in boiling water for 10 minutes and finely dice, discarding the tough stems.

Soften the vermicelli according to the instructions on the packet, drain and roughly chop.

Combine the mushrooms and noodles with the remaining filling ingredients and stir thoroughly, seasoning with salt and pepper.

Soak a rice paper wrapper in warm water for 1–2 minutes until pliable, remove and add another to soak. Place a generous spoonful of the mixture in the centre of the paper and roll up to form a cigar, tucking in the ends as you go. Place seam-side down on a plate and repeat until all the papers and filling are used up. Cover with a damp tea towel if not serving immediately. Serve with the chilli sauce.

*If you are using the 20cm size rice papers, allow 40g of mixture per roll; if using the 16cm size, allow 30g per roll. If you have an electric set of scales you might consider putting the paper on the scales, setting to zero and then proceeding with the measured mixture.*

# prawn and mango rolls

makes 20–25 rolls

500g cooked, peeled prawns
1 mango, peeled and diced
zest and juice of 1 lime
2 tablespoons fish sauce (*nam pla*)
2 teaspoons light brown sugar
large handful of beansprouts
small bunch of Thai basil, leaves
    picked and roughly chopped
small bunch of mint, leaves picked
    and roughly chopped
salt and white pepper

20 x 20cm or 25 x 16cm rice
    paper wrappers

Combine all the filling ingredients, season with salt and pepper and toss to mix.

Soak a rice paper in warm water for 1–2 minutes until pliable, remove and add another to soak. Place a generous spoonful of the mixture in the centre of the paper and roll up to form a cigar, tucking in the ends as you go. Place seam-side down on a plate and repeat until all the papers and filling are used up. Cover with a damp tea towel if not serving immediately.

# seafood rolls

makes 30–40 pancakes

handful of beansprouts
2 tablespoons finely diced fennel
1 head little gem lettuce, finely
    shredded
2 tablespoons finely sliced
    spring onion
3cm piece of ginger root, peeled
    and grated
2 garlic cloves, peeled and finely
    chopped
1 tablespoon fish sauce (*nam pla*)
1 tablespoon soy sauce
1 teaspoon toasted sesame oil
1 red chilli, peeled and finely diced
bunch of coriander, leaves picked
juice of 1 lime
400g cooked, peeled prawns
500g cooked and picked crabmeat
    (at least 50 per cent
    brown meat)
salt and white pepper

20cm or 16cm rice paper wrappers

Combine all the filling ingredients, season well with salt and pepper and toss well to mix.

Soak a rice paper in warm water for 1–2 minutes until pliable, remove and add another to soak. Place a generous spoonful of the mixture in the centre of the paper and roll up to form a cigar, tucking in the ends as you go. Place seam-side down on a plate and repeat until all the papers and filling are used up. Cover with a damp tea towel if not serving immediately.

# prawn salad rolls

makes about 8

for the dressing
zest and juice of 1 lime
1 teaspoon fish sauce (*nam pla*)
1 teaspoon hoisin sauce
1 chilli, deseeded and finely sliced
1 garlic clove, peeled and minced

for the rolls
100g cooked, peeled prawns
handful of beansprouts
50g frozen peas, defrosted
1 medium carrot, julienned
2 tablespoons roughly chopped
    coriander
2 teaspoons sesame seeds, briefly
    toasted in a hot, dry frying pan

16cm Vietnamese rice paper
    wrappers
sweet chilli dipping sauce (see
    page 16)

Combine all the dressing ingredients and set aside.

Combine the prawns, beansprouts, peas, carrot, coriander and sesame seeds in a separate bowl. Pour over the dressing and mix well.

Dip the wrappers one by one in a bowl of hot water for about 30 seconds. Remove and lay on a board to soften. Place a generous spoonful of the salad mixture in the centre of a wrapper, and fold one side of the paper over. Tuck in each end and then roll over to seal the final side. Place seam-side down on a plate and repeat with the other wrappers. Cover with a damp tea towel if not using immediately.

Transfer the rolls to a large serving plate or divide between individual dishes. Serve with sweet chilli sauce for dipping.

30g dried Chinese mushrooms

200g minced chicken

2 garlic cloves, peeled and finely
    chopped

3cm piece of ginger root, peeled
    and grated

100g Chinese cabbage, finely sliced

1 tablespoon soy sauce

1 tablespoon *mirin* (see page 11)

2 tablespoons finely chopped
    spring onion

1 tablespoon toasted sesame oil

1 red chilli, finely diced

1 tablespoon fish sauce (*nam pla*)

½ teaspoon sugar

100g water chestnuts, finely diced

salt and white pepper

60 wonton skins

vegetable oil

*gyoza* sauce (see page 23)

# mushroom and chicken gyozas

Soak the mushrooms in boiling water for 10 minutes and finely slice, discarding the tough stems. Add to the rest of the filling ingredients and mix well. It is best to do this using your hands: as you work the meat will absorb the liquid. Season well with salt and pepper.

Put a teaspoonful of the mixture in the centre of each wonton skin. Moisten the edges with a little water and then fold over to create a half-moon shape. Press down to form a seal.

Heat a large frying pan over a medium heat for 1–2 minutes, or until hot and almost smoking, and add 1 tablespoon of oil. Reduce the heat to moderate, put 4–6 dumplings in the pan and sauté gently for 1 minute each side or until just starting to brown. Don't overcrowd the pan or they will stew.

Remove the pan from the heat, add 3 tablespoons water and cover immediately with a lid or aluminium foil. Return to the heat for 1 minute, then remove and set aside for a further 2 minutes, by which time the *gyozas* will be heated through. Repeat for the remaining *gyozas*. It is quicker if you can use two pans, starting to heat the second one just before adding the water to the first pan.

Serve with the *gyoza* sauce. Ideally, serve one batch while you prepare the next because they are best warm.

# pork gyozas

**makes about 80**

150g Chinese cabbage, finely
    chopped
50g bamboo shoots, finely chopped
450g minced pork
1 tablespoon soy sauce
1 tablespoon fish sauce (*nam pla*)
1 tablespoon *mirin* (see page 11)
2 tablespoons finely chopped
    shallots
3cm piece of ginger root, peeled
    and grated
1 tablespoon seasame seeds,
    briefly toasted in a hot, dry
    frying pan
1 tablespoon roughly chopped
    coriander
½ teaspoon sugar
1 egg, lightly beaten
1 red chilli, deseeded and finely
    chopped
salt and white pepper

80 wonton skins
vegetable oil
*gyoza* sauce (see page 23)

Put all the ingredients for the filling in a bowl and mix together. It is best to do this with your hands. Thoroughly season with salt and pepper.

Put a teaspoonful of the mixture in the centre of each wonton skin. Moisten the edges with a little water and then fold over to create a half-moon shape. Press down to form a seal.

Heat a large frying pan over a medium heat for 1–2 minutes, or until hot and almost smoking and add 1 tablespoon of vegetable oil. Reduce the heat to moderate, put 4–6 dumplings in the pan and sauté gently for 1 minute each side or until just starting to brown. Don't overcrowd the pan or they will stew.

Remove the pan from the heat, add 3 tablespoons water and cover immediately with a lid or with aluminium foil. Return to the heat for 1 minute, then remove and set aside for a further 2 minutes, by which time the *gyozas* will be heated through. Repeat for the remaining *gyozas*. It is quicker if you can use two pans, starting to heat the second just before adding the water to the first pan.

Serve with the *gyoza* sauce.

gamama

# quick

Fast food takes on a new meaning with noodles. Here you have healthy ingredients. Fresh too. Combined in, at most, 10 minutes. Altogether a different proposition to some fast food we could mention. When you eat a noodle dish at wagamama the only pre-cooked part is the noodles. After that, what you eat is cooked only when you order it. We like the discipline. We also like the result.

This is why we deliver food when it is cooked. That way we feel you get the best. This is important when you want to eat something nutritious. It also tastes better.

None of the dishes in this book takes that long. Just like in the restaurants, the aim is really to get food on the table in a matter of minutes rather than hours. This chapter, however, contains the super-charged recipes. Those that come at you so that you are caught unawares. Supper in seconds you might say.

It might not seem that fast as you chop away with no heat in sight. But this is the way with noodles. A hot wok will wilt pak choi in moments, seal chicken in seconds, render a scallop a deeply golden caramelised colour in no time. Well, very little time.

The secret to this really fast noodle cooking lies in choosing ingredients that need very little heat to give their best and which are suitably cut. So take care on the board.

There are often times when we want food fast. Not always, but certainly occasionally. There is every reason why the care taken should be just the same as with more complicated dishes. Good food fast? Why not?

# chive and chilli noodles

serves 2

75g unsalted peanuts
100g medium egg noodles

**for the dressing**
1–2 red chillies (or to taste),
   deseeded and finely chopped
4 Chinese flowering chives (see
   page 11), finely chopped
2 teaspoons rice vinegar
zest and juice of ½ lemon

2 tablespoons vegetable oil
1 red onion, peeled and chopped
1 garlic clove, peeled and crushed
1 red pepper, deseeded and
   thinly sliced
125g courgette, sliced
handful of baby spinach

Preheat the oven to 200°C/gas mark 6 and roast the peanuts on a tray for 5–6 minutes or until just coloured. Transfer to a cold plate and allow to cool. Roughly chop.

Cook the noodles according to the instructions on the packet, drain and refresh under cold water.

To make the dressing, whisk together the chilli, chives, rice vinegar and lemon zest and juice. Set aside.

Heat the vegetable oil in a hot wok and stir fry the onion for 2–3 minutes until softened. Add the garlic, red pepper and courgette, stir fry for a further 4 minutes over a medium heat until lightly browned. Add the peanuts and cook for a further minute.

Add the noodles and spinach and toss through the vegetables until the noodles are hot and the spinach just wilted. Add the dressing and ensure that all ingredients are evenly coated. Check the seasoning and serve.

# spinach and soba noodles

serves 2

100g *soba* noodles
1 tablespoon vegetable oil
3 garlic cloves, peeled and mashed
3cm piece of ginger root, peeled
    and grated
250g baby spinach, washed
1 tablespoon oyster sauce
1 tablespoon toasted sesame oil
juice of 1 lime
2 teaspoons sesame seeds, briefly
    toasted in a hot, dry frying pan
1 chilli, deseeded and finely
    chopped

Cook the noodles according to the instructions on the packet, drain and refresh under cold water.

Heat the oil in a hot wok and stir fry the garlic, ginger and spinach for 2 minutes. Add the noodles, toss once, remove from the heat and stir in the oyster sauce and sesame oil.

Squeeze over the lime juice and serve with the sesame seeds and chilli scattered over the top.

# spiced vegetable noodles

serves 2

100g thin rice vermicelli
1 tablespoon vegetable oil
2 garlic cloves, peeled and finely
    chopped
3cm piece of ginger root, peeled
    and grated
2 lemongrass stalks, outer leaves
    removed, finely chopped
1 tablespoon finely chopped
    shallots
2 red chillies, finely chopped
1 teaspoon curry powder
handful of finely sliced little
    gem lettuce
1 cucumber, deseeded and cut
    into batons
handful of mangetout, sliced
    lengthways
1 tablespoon soy sauce
scant ½ teaspoon soft brown sugar
salt and pepper

Cook the vermicelli according to the instructions on the packet, drain and refresh under cold water.

Add the vegetable oil to a hot wok and stir fry the garlic, ginger, lemongrass, shallots and chillies for 1 minute. Add the curry powder, lettuce, cucumber and mangetout and stir fry for 5 minutes or until the vegetables are cooked, but still crunchy.

Add the soy sauce, sugar and noodles and toss so everything is well coated. Season with salt and pepper and serve.

# red pepper and pak choi with spiced udon noodles

serves 2

150g *udon* noodles
2 garlic cloves, peeled and minced
1 tablespoon dried shrimps, soaked
    in hot water, drained and
    chopped
3cm piece of ginger root, peeled
    and sliced
2 lemongrass stalks, outer leaves
    removed, finely chopped
1 tablespoon finely chopped red
    onion
bunch of coriander
3 tablespoons vegetable oil
1 red pepper, deseeded and very
    thinly sliced
1 head pak choi, roughly chopped
1–2 chillies (or to taste),
    finely chopped

Cook the noodles according to the instructions on the packet, drain and refresh under cold water.

Combine all the other ingredients except the oil, red pepper, pak choi and chilli in a pestle and mortar and grind to a paste. Stir in 2 tablespoons of the oil.

Heat the remaining tablespoon of oil in a hot wok. Add the prepared paste and stir fry for 2 minutes or until it loses its raw flavour. Add the vegetables and carry on cooking for a further 2 minutes. Add the noodles to the wok and toss so that everything is well coated.

Check the seasoning and serve sprinkled with the chilli.

# quick vegetable noodles

serves 2

100g flat egg noodles
1 tablespoon vegetable oil
2 chillies, deseeded and finely diced
2 garlic cloves, peeled and finely
    chopped
3cm piece of ginger root, peeled
    and grated
1 red onion, peeled and cut
    vertically into eighths
100g runner beans, trimmed and
    sliced into 6cm lengths
1 red pepper, deseeded and
    sliced lengthways
1 tablespoon soy sauce
2 tablespoons sake
1 teaspoon soft brown sugar
1 tablespoon oyster sauce

Cook the noodles according to the instructions on the packet, drain and refresh under cold water.

Heat the oil in a hot wok and stir fry the chillies, garlic and ginger for 30 seconds. Add the vegetables and continue to stir fry for 5–6 minutes or until wilted, adding 1 tablespoon water half way through. Stir in the soy sauce, sake, sugar and oyster sauce along with the noodles. Toss so that everything is well coated and heated through, and serve.

150g *soba* noodles

1 teaspoon toasted sesame oil

2 tablespoons rice vinegar

1 tablespoon soy sauce

2 teaspoons light brown sugar

scant teaspoon Chinese chilli paste
  (available from Oriental stores)

1 tablespoon vegetable oil

250g raw, peeled tiger prawns,
  deveined and roughly chopped

2 spring onions, finely sliced

3cm piece of root ginger, peeled
  and finely chopped

1 garlic clove, peeled and crushed

few coriander leaves

# chilli prawns with soba noodles

Cook the noodles according to the instructions on the packet, drain, then return to the pot and toss with the sesame oil.

In a small bowl combine the rice vinegar, soy sauce, sugar and chilli paste.

Heat the oil in a hot wok and stir fry the prawns, spring onions, ginger and garlic for 1–2 minutes.

Add the chilli mixture to the wok and cook for 1 minute. Add the noodles and toss so that everything is well coated and heated through. Scatter over the coriander.

100g *udon* noodles

1 tablespoon vegetable oil

3cm piece of ginger root, peeled and grated

2 garlic cloves, peeled and minced with a little salt

pinch of Chinese five-spice

1 tablespoon black bean sauce

6–8 scallops

2 handfuls of baby spinach

bunch of mint, leaves picked

50ml chicken stock (see page 13)

1 tablespoon soy sauce

pinch of sugar

2 teaspoons toasted sesame oil

2 teaspoons sweet chilli dipping sauce (see page 16)

2 spring onions, finely sliced

# spiced scallops with spinach, mint and sweet chilli dressing

Cook the noodles according to the instructions on the packet, drain and refresh under cold water.

Heat the oil in a hot wok and stir fry the ginger, garlic, five-spice, black bean sauce and scallops for 2 minutes. Add the spinach and mint leaves, stock, soy sauce, sugar and sesame oil and simmer for 1 minute, or until reduced slightly. Check the seasoning. Add the noodles and toss everything so that it is well coated and heated through.

Serve drizzled with the sweet chilli dipping sauce and topped with the spring onions.

# soy-braised salmon

serves 2

100g flat Chinese noodles
5 dried shiitake mushrooms
1 tablespoon vegetable oil
1 onion, peeled and finely chopped
1 carrot, peeled and thinly sliced
2 garlic cloves, peeled and crushed
3cm piece of ginger root, peeled
    and grated
200g salmon, cut into 3cm squares
2 tablespoons soy sauce
100ml chicken stock (see
    page 13)
2 teaspoons cornflour, dissolved in
    2 tablespoons water
salt and white pepper

Cook the noodles according to the instructions on the packet, drain and refresh under cold water. Soak the mushrooms in 125ml boiling water.

Heat the oil in a hot wok and stir fry the onion, carrot, garlic, ginger and salmon for 1 minute. Add the soy sauce, cover, turn the heat down and simmer for 2 minutes.

Drain the mushrooms, reserving the liquid. Remove and discard the tough stalks and finely slice. Add the chicken stock to the pan with the mushrooms, reserved liquid and dissolved cornflour. Bring to the boil, add the noodles, tossing to combine and taking care not to break up the salmon too much. Taste and season with salt and pepper and serve.

# salmon and pak choi noodles

serves 2

for the marinade
1 tablespoon soy sauce
1 tablespoon sake
2 garlic cloves, peeled and minced
3cm piece of ginger root, peeled
    and grated

100g *somen* noodles
1 tablespoon vegetable oil
100g skinless salmon fillet or cutlets,
    cut into bite-sized pieces
2 pak choi, quartered lengthways
1 teaspoon cornflour mixed with a
    little cold water
2 tablespoons soy sauce
600ml chicken stock (see page 13)
2 tablespoons sake

To make the marinade, combine the ingredients, add the salmon and toss gently so the pieces are well coated. Set aside for 1 hour; overnight in the fridge is even better.

Cook the noodles according to the instructions on the packet, drain and refresh under cold water.

Heat the oil in a hot wok and stir fry the salmon and pak choi for 2 minutes. Blend the cornflour with the soy sauce and add to the wok with the chicken stock and sake. Simmer until everything has thickened and the fish is cooked, about 3–4 minutes.

Toss the noodles through and serve.

100g medium egg noodles

1 teaspoon cornflour

1 tablespoon soy sauce

2 tablespoons vegetable oil

150g boneless dark chicken meat
(leg or thigh), cut into bite-
sized pieces

1 green pepper, deseeded and cut
into 3cm pieces

2 tablespoons fermented black
beans, rinsed and roughly
chopped

4 garlic cloves, peeled and finely
chopped

3cm piece of ginger root, peeled
and minced

1 chilli, deseeded and finely
chopped

600ml chicken stock (see page 13)

1 tablespoon sake

# chicken and egg noodles with black bean sauce

Cook the noodles according to the instructions on the packet, drain and refresh under cold water.

Blend the cornflour with the soy sauce.

Heat a wok and when hot add the vegetable oil. Add the chicken and green pepper and stir fry for 2 minutes. Add the black beans, garlic, ginger and chilli and continue cooking for a further 3–4 minutes or until the chicken has almost cooked.

Stir in the chicken stock, blended cornflour and sake. Simmer for 2 minutes.

Spoon the noodles on to 2 plates, and serve topped with the chicken and black bean sauce.

serves 2

150g *soba* noodles

500ml chicken stock (see page 13)

1 leek, white part only, thinly sliced

2 tablespoons soy sauce

2 teaspoons fish sauce (*nam pla*)

1 tablespoon sake

150g boneless chicken breast, cut
into bite-sized pieces

2 handfuls of baby spinach leaves,
washed and roughly chopped

2 teaspoons sesame seeds, briefly
toasted in a hot, dry frying pan

# chicken, spinach and soba noodle soup

Cook the noodles according to the instructions on the packet, drain and refresh under cold water.

Bring the chicken stock to the boil, add the leek, soy sauce, fish sauce and sake. Cook for 10 minutes or until the leek softens. Turn the heat down, add the chicken and poach gently for 4–5 minutes or until cooked. Add the spinach, bring back to the boil and remove from the heat.

Divide the noodles equally between 2 bowls and ladle over the spinach, chicken and broth. Sprinkle with the sesame seeds and serve.

# stir-fried chicken noodles

for the marinade
2 tablespoons soy sauce
2 tablespoons *mirin* (see page 11)
1 teaspoon sugar

100g chicken thigh meat, cut into
    bite-sized pieces
salt and white pepper
100g medium egg noodles
1 tablespoon vegetable oil
2 garlic cloves, peeled and finely
    chopped
½ red pepper, deseeded and
    finely sliced
handful of mangetout, thinly sliced
    lengthways
2 teaspoons toasted sesame oil
2 teaspoons sesame seeds, briefly
    toasted in a hot, dry frying pan
bunch of coriander, leaves picked

Combine the marinade ingredients in a bowl, add the chicken and toss well to coat the pieces. Season with salt and pepper and set aside for 1 hour; overnight in the fridge is even better.

Drain the chicken, reserving the marinade.

Cook the noodles according to the instructions on the packet, drain and refresh under cold water.

Heat the vegetable oil in a hot wok and stir fry the garlic for 30 seconds. Add the chicken, stir fry for 2 minutes, then add the red pepper, mangetout and reserved marinade and stir fry for a further 2 minutes. Add the noodles and sesame oil and toss so that everything is well coated and heated through. Check the seasoning.

Serve with a sprinkling of the sesame seeds and coriander.

## chicken fried noodles with sausage

serves 2

100g Thai-style rice noodles

2 tablespoons vegetable oil

1 egg, beaten and seasoned

2 garlic cloves, peeled and finely
    chopped

1 red chilli, deseeded and finely
    chopped

100g chicken breast, cut into bite-
    sized pieces

50g firm pork sausage, sliced

1 head pak choi, roughly sliced
    lengthways

1 teaspoon soft brown sugar

1 tablespoon soy sauce

handful of beansprouts

60g kamaboko-aka (see
    page 11), sliced

2 spring onions, finely sliced

Cook the noodles according to the instructions on the packet, drain and refresh under cold water.

Put 1 tablespoon of the vegetable oil into a hot wok. Add the egg, swirl so that it coats the base and cook for 1 minute. Remove, allow to cool, then roll up and thinly slice.

Add the remaining tablespoon of oil to the wok and stir fry the garlic and chilli for 30 seconds. Add the chicken, sausage and pak choi. Stir fry for 3–4 minutes or until the chicken is cooked.

Add the sugar, soy sauce, beansprouts and kamaboko-aka along with the reserved noodles and the egg and toss so that everything is heated through.

Serve topped with the spring onions.

## stir-fried chicken and mushrooms with somen noodles

serves 2

100g somen noodles

1 tablespoon vegetable oil

2 chicken breasts, cut into
    bite-sized slices

75g button mushrooms, thinly
    sliced

75g shiitake mushrooms, thinly
    sliced

3cm piece of ginger root, peeled
    and grated

2 garlic cloves, peeled and mashed

2 teaspoons soy sauce

1 tablespoon sake

1 tablespoon mirin (see page 11)

1 lime, cut into wedges

handful of coriander leaves

Cook the noodles according to the instructions on the packet, drain and refresh under cold water.

Heat the oil in a hot wok over a medium heat and stir fry the chicken, mushrooms, ginger and garlic for 2–3 minutes. Add the soy sauce, sake, mirin and 2 tablespoons water, continue to stir fry for 2 minutes or until the chicken is cooked.

Stir in the noodles to heat through and serve with a wedge of lime and a scattering of coriander leaves.

# pork and soba noodles

serves 2

200g pork fillet, thinly sliced
1 tablespoon *char siu* sauce
(Chinese barbecue sauce,
widely available)
½ teaspoon Chinese five-spice
¼ teaspoon cinnamon
2 tablespoons sake
100g thick *soba* noodles
1 tablespoon vegetable oil
60g flowering greens (*choy sum*)
50g button mushrooms, sliced
handful of beansprouts
½ red pepper, deseeded and finely
sliced
2 spring onions, finely sliced
2 tablespoons *yasai soba* dressing
(see page 16)
2 eggs, lightly beaten
1 tablespoon finely sliced *kimchee*
(see page 11)
2 teaspoons sesame seeds

Combine the pork, *char siu* sauce, Chinese five-spice, cinnamon and sake in a plastic bag and leave in the fridge overnight to marinate.

Cook the noodles according to the instructions on the packet, drain and refresh under cold water.

Heat the oil in a hot wok and add, one at a time, the noodles, pork, flowering greens, mushrooms, beansprouts, red pepper, spring onions, *yasai soba* dressing and eggs, tossing well and stir frying for a total of 6–7 minutes.

Serve sprinkled with the *kimchee* and sesame seeds.

*This recipe was created by Geraldo Suwu, from wagamama in Amsterdam.*

# stir-fried beef with broccoli

serves 2

150g medium egg noodles

100g broccoli, broken into small
    florets

2 tablespoons vegetable oil

150g beef sirloin, thinly sliced into
    bite-sized pieces

2 garlic cloves, peeled and mashed

3cm piece of ginger root, peeled
    and grated

1 tablespoon soy sauce

1 tablespoon fish sauce (*nam pla*)

Cook the noodles according to the instructions on the packet, drain and refresh under cold water.

Blanch the broccoli for 2–3 minutes in boiling salted water, drain and refresh under cold water.

Heat the oil in a hot wok over a medium heat and stir fry the beef, garlic and ginger for 3–4 minutes or until the beef is almost cooked. Add the noodles, broccoli, soy sauce and fish sauce. Toss so that everything is well combined and heated through.

Check the seasoning and serve.

# sweet and sour
# beef noodles

serves 2

100g medium egg noodles

1 tablespoon vegetable oil

2 garlic cloves, peeled and finely
    chopped

3cm piece of ginger root, peeled
    and finely chopped

150g beef steak (sirloin is
    probably best), cut into
    thin strips

½ red pepper, deseeded and
    finely sliced

2 teaspoons cornflour

2 tablespoons soy sauce

1 teaspoon sugar

100ml chicken stock (see page 13)

1 tablespoon *mirin* (see page 11)

1 tablespoon rice vinegar

juice of 1 lime

2 tablespoons frozen peas,
    defrosted

handful of beansprouts

bunch of coriander, leaves picked

2 spring onions, finely sliced

Cook the noodles according to the instructions on the packet, drain and refresh under cold water.

Heat the oil in a hot wok and stir fry the garlic and ginger for 30 seconds. Add the beef, toss well and then add the red pepper, stir frying for 3 minutes. Blend the cornflour with the soy sauce and add, along with the sugar, chicken stock, *mirin* and rice vinegar. Toss so that everything is well coated and simmer for 1 minute to thicken slightly. Add the noodles, lime juice, peas and beansprouts. Cook everything for a further 3 minutes.

Serve scattered with the coriander and spring onions.

# entertaining

Entertaining with noodles really is a doddle. No complicated cooking, just good clean flavours. The preparation is easy, the cooking is quick and hassle-free and the serving amounts to little more than a few bowls. You can get your friends to help or do it all beforehand — nothing could be simpler. Any cooking is done at the last minute, which means you remain in control.

Noodle stalls in Asia are based on the same principle: advance preparation = speed of service. You chop, precook the noodles, and hold. Wait for everyone to arrive and then magically it all appears. The secret lies in doing enough, but not too much. Nobody wants to reheat things when stir frying is so quick.

Sharing food is such an important part of entertaining and these kinds of dishes are perfect for communal eating. A lettuce leaf stuffed with scallops and noodles to start perhaps, and then, when you sit down, salmon teriyaki with *soba* noodle salad, or Thai-style prawns with peanuts and chilli, or beef and black bean sauce with egg noodles.

A salad or two might bring everything to a refreshing conclusion. Offer a summer salad with pickled ginger (*gari*) on warm days, or marinated mushroom salad with cellophane noodles for when the weather is a little more inclement.

This is cooking to be done out in front of your guests, cooking to be proud of, cooking to be enjoyed with the minimum of fuss and the maximum of taste, texture and flavour. Fast food of the right kind.

50g rice vermicelli, broken into
6cm lengths
vegetable oil
12 scallops, sliced in half
horizontally
1 garlic clove, peeled and mashed
3cm piece of ginger root, peeled
and grated
1 tablespoon soy sauce
1 tablespoon hoisin sauce
salt and white pepper
12 little gem lettuce leaves
½ cucumber, deseeded and cut
into matchsticks
handful of beansprouts
1 tablespoon crispy fried shallots
(available from Oriental stores),
optional
lime wedges
soy dipping sauce (see page 22)

# stuffed lettuce leaves with scallops, noodles and soy dipping sauce

Cook the vermicelli according to the instructions on the packet, drain and refresh under cold water.

Heat a little oil in a hot wok and stir fry the scallops for 2 minutes, or until they just colour. Add the garlic and ginger and stir fry for a further minute. Add the soy and hoisin sauces and the drained noodles. Season with salt and pepper and remove from the heat.

To serve, arrange the lettuce leaves on a large plate. Place 2 scallop halves in each lettuce leaf along with some noodles. Top with the cucumber and beansprouts, crispy fried shallots and a wedge of lime for squeezing.

Serve with the soy dipping sauce on the side.

serves 2

100g egg noodles
2 tablespoons vegetable oil
handful of baby corn
1 red pepper, deseeded and cut
into strips
1 small head broccoli, broken
into florets
1 heaped tablespoon green curry
paste (see page 18)
200ml coconut milk (half a tin)
200g tinned bamboo shoots,
drained and rinsed
handful of mangetout
handful of coriander leaves

# green curry noodles

Cook the noodles according to the instructions on the packet, drain and refresh under cold water.

Heat the oil in a hot wok and stir fry the baby corn, red pepper and broccoli for 5 minutes or until they just start to colour. Add the green chilli paste and cook for a further minute or until it loses its raw flavour. Add the coconut milk and 100ml water, together with the bamboo shoots and mangetout. Cook for 2 minutes.

Add the noodles to the wok and toss them thoroughly so that everything is well combined.

Check the seasoning and serve sprinkled with the coriander leaves.

# somen noodle shrimps with sweet ginger dip

serves 3–4

**for the sweet ginger dip**

2 tablespoons soy sauce

1 teaspoon fish sauce (*nam pla*)

1 tablespoon sugar

3cm piece of ginger root, peeled
    and grated


100g *somen* noodles, broken into
    6cm lengths

12 raw tiger prawns, peeled but tail
    on, deveined and seasoned

1 sheet of *nori* seaweed, cut into
    12 strips, 9cm long

vegetable oil, for deep frying


bamboo skewers

To make the dip, combine the soy sauce, fish sauce, sugar and ginger in a saucepan, bring to the boil and simmer for 3 minutes or until just thickening. Strain and allow to cool.

Cover the noodles with boiling water and soak for 2 minutes, drain thoroughly and pat dry with a clean tea towel.

Push a skewer down each prawn from the tail end towards the head. Place a strip of seaweed on a board. Lay a pinch of noodles about the same width as the prawn at right angles to the seaweed. Place a skewered prawn on top of the noodles. Moisten the visible part of the seaweed and roll up to seal so it forms a band around the noodles and prawn. Repeat with each prawn.

Pour the oil to a depth of 4cm in a suitable pan. Heat over a medium-high heat. When hot, drop in the prawns in batches and cook for 3 minutes, turning occasionally, or until the noodles are crispy and golden brown.

Drain on kitchen paper and serve with the sweet ginger dip.

# thai-style prawns with peanuts and chilli

serves 2


100g wide Thai-style rice noodles

2 tablespoons vegetable oil

1 tablespoon red curry paste
    (see page 16)

12 large raw, peeled prawns

2 garlic cloves, peeled and crushed

2 small pak choi, sliced lengthways

handful of frozen peas, defrosted

6 baby corn

small bunch of coriander, stems
    chopped finely, leaves reserved

100ml soya milk

juice of 1 lime

1 tablespoon fish sauce (*nam pla*)

2 teaspoons light brown sugar

salt and white pepper

1 tablespoon roasted peanuts

Cook the noodles according to the instructions on the packet, drain and refresh under cold water.

Heat the vegetable oil in a wok and when hot add the curry paste, stir fry for 2 minutes and then add the prawns and garlic. Cook until the prawns start to lose their raw colour, about 4 minutes. Transfer to a bowl and set aside.

Add the pak choi, peas, baby corn and coriander stems to the wok and stir fry for 3–4 minutes or until the vegetables start to wilt and colour.

Return the prawn mixture along with the soya milk, lime juice, fish sauce and sugar. Season with salt and pepper, add the noodles and cook for 3–4 minutes.

Serve with a scattering of peanuts and reserved coriander leaves.

2 salmon fillets

3 tablespoons soy sauce

3 tablespoons *mirin* (see page 11)

150g *udon* noodles

1 red chilli (or to taste), finely
    chopped

2 spring onions, finely chopped

large handful of baby spinach leaves

bunch of coriander, leaves picked
    and stems finely chopped

1 tablespoon vegetable oil

2 teaspoons sesame seeds, briefly
    toasted in a hot, dry frying pan

1 lime

sweet chilli dipping sauce (see
    page 16)

**for the dressing**

2 teaspoons toasted sesame oil

2 teaspoons dark soy sauce

juice of 1 lime

# salmon teriyaki with udon noodle salad

Combine the salmon, soy sauce and *mirin* in a shallow bowl, toss so they are well coated and marinate for 2 hours; overnight in the fridge is even better.

Cook the noodles according to the instructions on the packet, drain and refresh briefly under cold water, they still want to be warm.

Combine the dressing ingredients in a large bowl and toss the noodles through. Add the chilli, spring onions, spinach and coriander and toss well. Divide between 2 plates.

Heat the oil in a frying pan. Remove the salmon from the marinade, season with salt and pepper and sear, skin-side down for 2 minutes. Turn over and fry on the other side for 2 minutes. Turn back on to the skin side and cook for a further 2 minutes or until the skin is crisp.

Place the salmon (skin-side up) on the noodles, top with the sesame seeds and serve with half a lime and the chilli dipping sauce.

serves 2

for the marinade

1 teaspoon cornflour

3cm piece of ginger root, peeled
    and grated

2 garlic cloves, peeled and grated

2 teaspoons soy sauce

2 teaspoons oyster sauce

1 tablespoon vegetable oil

200g monkfish, cut into pieces
    4cm long, 2cm thick

salt and white pepper

100g medium egg noodles

1 tablespoon vegetable oil

1 teaspoon cornflour

1 teaspoon soy sauce

pinch of light soft brown sugar

1 teaspoon oyster sauce

1 teaspoon toasted sesame oil

50ml chicken stock (see page 13)

large bunch of coriander, stems
    trimmed at the base but
    otherwise intact

1 tablespoon finely sliced spring
    onion

# monkfish and coriander with chinese noodles

Combine the marinade ingredients in a bowl, then add the monkfish pieces, tossing to coat thoroughly. Add a seasoning of salt and pepper. Set aside for 1 hour; overnight in the fridge is even better.

Cook the noodles according to the instructions on the packet, drain and refresh under cold water.

Heat the oil in a hot wok and stir fry the monkfish and its marinade for 3–4 minutes or until the fish is cooked. Blend the cornflour with the soy sauce, sugar and oyster sauce. Add to the wok with the sesame oil and chicken stock and simmer for 30 seconds. Add the coriander and continue cooking for a further 30 seconds until the coriander wilts. Add the noodles and toss so that everything is combined and heated through. Remove from the heat, and check the seasoning.

Serve sprinkled with the spring onion.

*Coriander is undoubtedly a strong herb but there are times when using it to excess really pays off. Here it is used almost like a vegetable.*

# marinated quail with stir-fried noodles

for the marinade

1 tablespoon soy sauce

1 garlic clove, peeled and minced

2 teaspoons honey

1 tablespoon *mirin* (see page 11)

1 teaspoon fish sauce (*nam pla*)

2 teaspoons lime juice

2 quail, spatchcocked (see note below)

125g fresh egg noodles (or 75g dried)

3 tablespoons vegetable oil

75g field mushrooms, sliced

75g mangetout

8 baby corn, halved lengthways

3cm piece of ginger root, peeled and grated

2 teaspoons soy sauce

2 teaspoons cornflour

100ml chicken stock (see page 13)

1 tablespoon oyster sauce

1 tablespoon *mirin* (see page 11)

Combine the marinade ingredients in a large bowl and stir gently but thoroughly to amalgamate everything. Add the quail and coat thoroughly.

Cook the noodles according to the instructions on the packet, drain and refresh under cold water.

Heat the vegetable oil in a hot wok. Brush the marinade off the quail (reserving the marinade) and sear for 5–6 minutes on each side over a medium–low heat (too hot and you will burn the marinade), or until well coloured and cooked through. Remove from the wok and keep warm. Wipe out the wok, add the reserved marinade, the mushooms, mangetout, baby corn and ginger and stir fry for 2–3 minutes over a high heat.

Combine the soy sauce and cornflour. Add to the wok with the remaining ingredients, stirring to avoid lumps forming. Once everything starts to bubble, add the noodles and toss to ensure that everything is well coated.

Transfer to a serving dish, top with the quail and serve.

*Spatchcock the quail by cutting down either side of the backbone, which should be discarded. Place the quail, breast side up, on a board and press down firmly to flatten – you need to break the breastbone so the birds stay flat.*

# chicken and prawn hot-pot

12 raw, peeled tiger prawns,
    deveined
150g boneless, skinless dark
    chicken meat (leg or thigh),
    roughly chopped
6 shiitake mushrooms, stems
    removed, roughly chopped
5 Chinese cabbage leaves, sliced
1 carrot, julienned
2 heads baby pak choi, roughly
    chopped
handful of mangetout, trimmed
3cm piece of ginger root, peeled
    and grated
200g *udon* noodles
1 litre chicken stock (see page 13)
1 tablespoon soy sauce
1 tablespoon *mirin* (see page 11)
salt and white pepper
2 spring onions, finely sliced

Arrange the prawns, chicken, mushrooms, cabbage leaves, carrots, pak choi, mangetout and ginger in a casserole dish just large enough to take all the ingredients. Place the noodles on top.

In a separate pan bring the stock to the boil, add the soy sauce and *mirin* and season with salt and pepper. Pour the stock over the ingredients and bring to a slow boil over a medium heat. Allow to simmer until all the ingredients are cooked, about 5 minutes.

Allow to rest for 2 minutes and serve from the casserole, sprinkled with the spring onions.

# crispy chicken noodles

100g medium egg noodles
300ml plus 2 tablespoons
    vegetable oil
1 tablespoon red curry paste
    (see page 16)
100g dark chicken meat (leg or
    thigh), coarsely chopped
2 pak choi, halved lengthways
small bunch of coriander, stems
    finely chopped, leaves reserved
1 tablespoon chopped shallots
salt and white pepper
100ml chicken stock (see
    page 13)
100ml coconut milk
2 teaspoons fish sauce (*nam pla*)
2 handfuls of beansprouts
1 red chilli, thinly sliced
1 tablespoon mint leaves
juice of 1 lime

Cook the noodles according to the instructions on the packet, drain and refresh under cold water. Add 1 tablespoon of the oil and toss to mix.

Heat the 300ml oil in a small pan or wok until it is hot enough to make a piece of noodle fluff up. Working in small batches, cook the noodles until crispy, drain on kitchen paper and transfer to 2 plates.

Heat the remaining tablespoon of oil in a hot wok. Add the red curry paste and fry for 30 seconds or until it loses its raw aroma (do not allow it to catch and burn). Add the chicken, pak choi, coriander stems and shallots, season with salt and stir fry for 3 minutes. Add the chicken stock, bring to the boil, lower the heat and add the coconut milk and fish sauce. Simmer for 10 minutes, or until the meat is cooked. Check the seasoning.

Combine the beansprouts, chilli, mint and reserved coriander leaves in a bowl and mix well.

To serve, spoon the chicken mixture on top of the crispy noodles, top with the beansprout mixture and drizzle with lime juice.

125g *soba* noodles

1 tablespoon vegetable oil

200g duck breast, skinned and
	thinly sliced

salt and white pepper

2 garlic cloves, peeled and thinly
	sliced

2 tablespoons frozen peas,
	defrosted

3 tablespoons *mirin* (see page 11)

2 tablespoons soy sauce

1 tablespoon bamboo shoots

bunch of mint, leaves picked

# stir-fried duck with soba noodles, peas and mint

Cook the noodles according to the instructions on the packet, drain and refresh under cold water.

Heat the oil in a hot wok. Season the duck with salt and pepper and stir fry for 3–4 minutes or until the meat is cooked.

Add the garlic, peas, *mirin* and soy sauce and continue to stir fry for 1 minute until everything looks glossy and reduced. Add the noodles, toss to ensure that everything is well combined. Taste and adjust the seasoning.

Divide between 2 bowls and serve scattered with the bamboo shoots and mint.

serves 2

125g *ramen* noodles

1 tablespoon vegetable oil

125g minced pork

6 button mushrooms, sliced

bunch of spring onions, cut into
	6cm lengths

100g raw, peeled prawns

2 red chillies, deseeded and
	finely sliced

2 garlic cloves, peeled and minced
	with a little salt

2 teaspoons muscovado sugar

1 tablespoon fish sauce (*nam pla*)

1 tablespoon rice vinegar

2 handfuls of beansprouts

2 tablespoons roughly chopped
	coriander leaves

1 lime, halved

# hot and sour pork and prawns with ramen noodles

Cook the noodles according to the instructions on the packet, drain and refresh under cold water.

Heat the oil in a hot wok and stir fry the pork for 3 minutes, then add the mushrooms, spring onions, prawns, chillies, garlic, sugar, fish sauce and rice vinegar. Stir fry for a further 3 minutes.

Add the noodles and toss to ensure that everything is well combined.

Divide between 2 bowls and serve topped with the beansprouts and coriander and a lime half to squeeze over.

# beef and black bean sauce with egg noodles

serves 2

125g medium egg noodles
1 tablespoon vegetable oil, plus
    extra for the noodles
2 teaspoons cornflour
100ml chicken stock (see page 13)
1 red onion, peeled and cut
    vertically into eighths
1 green pepper, deseeded and cut
    into 4cm squares
100g sirloin steak, finely sliced
2 garlic cloves, peeled and
    thinly sliced
4cm piece of ginger root, peeled
    and finely grated
1 tablespoon black bean sauce
1 red chilli, deseeded and finely
    sliced

Cook the noodles according to the instructions on the packet, drain and refresh under cold water. Toss with a little oil.

Dissolve the cornflour in 2 tablespoons of the chicken stock.

Heat the oil in a hot wok and stir fry the red onion and green pepper for 4 minutes. Add the sirloin, garlic and ginger and continue to stir fry for 1 minute. Add the black bean sauce, chilli, chicken stock and dissolved cornflour. Stir for 1 minute until the sauce thickens. Taste and adjust the seasoning.

Divide the noodles between 2 bowls. Pour over the beef mixture and serve.

# five-spice beef with rice noodles

serves 2

for the marinade
½ teaspoon Chinese five-spice
2 teaspoons oyster sauce
2 teaspoons soy sauce
1 tablespoon mirin (see page 11)
1 teaspoon cornflour

200g sirloin steak, thinly sliced
150g flat Thai-style rice noodles
2 teaspoons vegetable oil
3cm piece of ginger root, peeled
    and finely chopped
2 garlic cloves, peeled and finely
    chopped
1 red pepper, deseeded and cut
    into strips
2 teaspoons soy sauce
100ml chicken stock (see page 13)
2 spring onions, finely sliced

Combine the marinade ingredients in a large bowl. Add the steak, stir to coat thoroughly, and set aside for at least 1 hour; overnight in the fridge is even better.

Cook the noodles according to the instructions on the packet, drain and refresh under cold water.

Heat the oil in a hot wok and stir fry the ginger, garlic and red pepper for 2 minutes.

Add the beef, reserving the marinade. Stir fry for 2 minutes or until just cooked. Add the marinade along with the soy sauce and chicken stock. Simmer for 2 minutes, taste and check the seasoning, add the noodles and combine thoroughly.

Divide between 2 bowls and serve sprinkled with the spring onions.

for the *dashi*
10cm piece of *konbu* (kelp)
    seaweed
handful of dried bonito flakes
    (*katsuo bushi*, see page 11)

for the dipping sauce
3 tablespoons soy sauce
1 tablespoon lemon juice or *mirin*

100g egg noodles
200g beef sirloin, thinly sliced
4 shiitake mushrooms
100g enoki mushrooms
2 carrots, thinly sliced
2 spring onions, cut on the
    diagonal
handful of baby spinach
50g *kamaboko-aka* (see page 11),
    sliced 5mm thick
100g firm tofu, cubed

heating element to use at the table

# poached beef and noodles with mushrooms and tofu

Lightly brush the *konbu* with a damp cloth. Place in a saucepan and cover with 1 litre water. Bring to the boil. Remove from the heat, take out the *konbu* and discard. Add the bonito flakes, return to the heat and bring almost to the boil. Remove from the heat and wait for the bonito to sink to the bottom. Strain. If you leave the bonito in for too long it adds a bitter note. You have now made primary *dashi*.

Bring the *dashi* almost to the boil and transfer to the table over your heating element.

Combine the soy sauce and lemon juice to make the dipping sauce.

Cook the noodles according to the instructions on the packet, drain, refresh under cold water and transfer to a plate.

Arrange the meat, vegetables, *kamaboko-aka* and tofu in lines with the noodles at one end.

Each person then 'cooks' the various ingredients in the broth. The beef takes very little time, say a minute, while some of the vegetables take two or three minutes. Dip in the sauce and eat. When you have finished poaching all the ingredients pile the noodles into your bowl, ladle over the enriched *dashi* and eat as a soup.

*If you are in a hurry, you can skip making the primary* dashi *and use an instant version,* dashi no moto *(see page 11). A pan set over a nightlight or two makes a good heating element.*

# marinated beef skewers and egg noodles

serves 2

4 wooden skewers, soaked for 1 hour beforehand

for the marinade

1 lemongrass stalk, outer leaves removed, finely chopped

2 garlic cloves, peeled and minced

1 teaspoon sesame seeds, briefly toasted in a hot, dry frying pan

1 chilli, finely sliced

pinch of sugar

1 tablespoon soy sauce

2 teaspoons fish sauce (*nam pla*)

125g sirloin steak, trimmed and cut into strips

1cm piece of ginger root, peeled and grated

2 teaspoons oyster sauce

1 tablespoon *mirin* (see page 11)

2 teaspoons tahini paste

100g fresh egg noodles

25g roasted peanuts, roughly chopped

handful of coriander, leaves picked

handful of mint, leaves picked

6 Thai basil leaves

4 little gem lettuce leaves, roughly chopped

2 spring onions, finely sliced

Combine the marinade ingredients, taste, and season with salt and black pepper if required. Add the beef, mixing to coat well. (This part is important – if you simply toss the beef it will not take on as much flavour from the marinade.) Cover and set aside for an hour, or better still, place in the fridge overnight.

Thread the beef strips onto the soaked skewers, concertina style. Preheat the grill to high. Place the skewers on a tray under the grill and cook for 2 minutes each side; longer if you prefer your meat well done.

Combine the ginger, oyster sauce, *mirin* and tahini paste to make a thick dressing. Cook the noodles according to the instructions on the packet, drain, then return them to the pan and add the dressing and peanuts. Lightly toss to mix. You may need a little hot water if the paste is too thick.

Divide the noodles between 2 plates and top with the grilled meat skewers. Serve sprinkled with the coriander, mint, basil and lettuce leaves and spring onions.

## desserts

positive eating + positive living

14  **wild berry sorbet**                                              £2.75
    2 scoops of wild berry sorbet garnished with
    fresh blueberries and a sprig of mint

15  **lime and stem ginger tart**                                      £4.25
    a sweet pastry base filled with lime and stem
    ginger custard. served with crème fraiche and
    a twist of lime zest

16  *coconut reika*                                                    £2.95
    3 scoops of dairy coconut ice cream topped
    with fresh passion fruit sauce and toasted
    coconut flakes

17  **white chocolate and ginger cheesecake**                          £4.25
    creamy white chocolate and glacé stem ginger
    cheesecake on a crunchy ginger biscuit base
    topped with white chocolate shavings

18  *chocolate fudge cake*                                             £4.25
    rich chocolate fudge cake with a wasabi and
    white chocolate fudge filling. served with dairy
    vanilla ice cream

19  **natural fruit lollies**                                          £1.50
    ask your server for today's choice

* these desserts contain nuts and may contain traces of nuts

wagamama and positive eating + positive living are registered trademarks of wagamama limited

# one pot

Some dishes are more than soup, but not quite a stir fry. A little like a casserole or stew. Something hearty and warming. A bit of stir frying may be involved, but the finished dish tends to be in a pot, hence one-pot. Or one-wok as, confusingly, sometimes a wok is the best pot.

The dishes in this chapter tend to be of a robust nature. Lots of ingredients, lots of flavours, lots of attitude. Which is why we like them. Yet with so many items it is important to retain control.

One-pot cooking suits most of us. Minimal washing up for a start. But there is also a welcome simplicity. No sense of madness with multiple hot-plates on the go. We like a sense of calm and order in our kitchens. It is important.

One-pot cooking is very focused. It allows you to proceed in a very ordered way. Which is a good thing in a kitchen. Why complicate things when they don't need to be?

These dishes are meant to be shared at the table rather than plated up, as we do in the restaurants (or indeed as we suggest in many of the other chapters). That way you get to eat as you want. And a little more doesn't seem like a dramatic move. Or a little less for that matter.

These dishes are also a little slower than elsewhere in this book. There is more of an opportunity for ingredients to get to know each other. Whereas a stir fry comes hot off the pan, these dishes are far more mellow. Laid back even.

# stir-fried greens with plum sauce

serves 2

100g medium egg noodles
1 tablespoon vegetable oil
150g broccoli, broken into
    small florets
1 small onion, peeled and cut
    vertically into eighths
3cm piece of ginger root, peeled
    and finely grated
1 garlic clove, peeled and minced
1 pak choi, trimmed and leaves
    separated
2 tablespoons plum sauce
1 red chilli, deseeded and finely
    sliced
1 tablespoon soy sauce
100ml chicken stock (see
    page 13)
2 teaspoons cornflour dissolved
    in 2 tablespoons of the
    chicken stock
salt and white pepper

Cook the noodles according to the instructions on the packet, drain and refresh under cold water.

Heat the vegetable oil in a hot wok and stir fry the broccoli and onion for 2 minutes. Add the ginger, garlic, pak choi and toss well for 2–3 minutes. Add the plum sauce, chilli and soy sauce and cook for a further 2 minutes.

Add the chicken stock and dissolved cornflour and stir for 30 seconds until everything thickens, then add the noodles. Toss to ensure that everything is well coated, taste and adjust the seasoning and serve.

# stir-fried vegetables with cellophane noodles

serves 2

125g cellophane noodles
vegetable oil
1 green chilli, finely sliced
1 garlic clove, peeled and minced
1 teaspoon soft brown sugar
4 shiitake mushrooms, sliced
1 small carrot, julienned
1 red onion, peeled and cut into
    thin half-moon slices
½ Chinese cabbage, sliced
3 teaspoons soy sauce
juice of ½ lemon
2 teaspoons toasted sesame oil
1 tablespoon finely sliced spring
    onion

Soak the noodles in warm water until soft, about 5 minutes. Drain, refresh under cold water and roughly chop.

Add the vegetable oil to a hot wok over a medium heat and stir fry the chilli and garlic for 30 seconds. Add the sugar and cook for a further 30 seconds. Turn the heat up and add the mushrooms, carrot, red onion and Chinese cabbage. Stir fry for 3–4 minutes, or until the vegetables just start to colour.

Add the noodles and soy sauce and stir fry for a further 3 minutes or until the vegetables are just cooked. Remove from the heat, and add the lemon juice and sesame oil, tossing thoroughly to disperse evenly.

Serve sprinkled with the spring onion.

# braised summer vegetables with tofu

serves 2

2 tablespoons vegetable oil

150g firm tofu, cut into 3cm x 3cm x 1cm slices

1 tablespoon red curry paste (see page 16)

400ml chicken or vegetable stock (see page 13)

1 tablespoon soy sauce

2 teaspoons sake

100ml soya milk

2 yellow courgettes, cut into 0.5cm discs

50g frozen peas, defrosted

1 tablespoon finely sliced button mushrooms

2 teaspoons fish sauce (*nam pla*)

50g wide rice noodles

2 spring onions, green parts included, thinly sliced

Heat the oil in a hot wok and sauté the tofu for 2 minutes on each side, or until well coloured. Remove and set aside.

Pour off the oil and add the curry paste. Cook over a moderate heat for 1 minute or until it starts to lose its raw aroma. Add the stock, soy sauce, sake and soya milk, bring to the boil and add the vegetables and fish sauce. Cook over a moderate heat for 4 minutes or until the vegetables are just tender but with some bite.

Cook the noodles according to the instructions on the packet, drain and refresh under cold water.

Divide between 2 bowls. Return the tofu to the wok, check the seasoning and pour over the noodles. Serve scattered with the spring onions.

# teriyaki tofu steaks with glazed green vegetables

serves 4

100g cellophane noodles

2 tablespoons soy sauce

2 tablespoons *mirin* (see page 11)

2 tablespoons sake

1 teaspoon sugar

200g tofu, cut into steaks

2 shiitake mushrooms, sliced

1 garlic clove, finely chopped

100g broccoli florets, roughly chopped

1 leek, sliced and washed

100g pak choi, trimmed and roughly chopped

½ fennel bulb, thinly sliced

2 teaspoons cornflour, dissolved in 1 tablespoon water

1 teaspoon sesame seeds, briefly toasted in a hot, dry frying pan

Cook the noodles according to the instructions on the packet, drain and refresh under cold water. Heat the soy sauce, *mirin,* sake and sugar in a wok until the sugar dissolves. Add the tofu and mushrooms and simmer for 15 minutes.

Stir in the garlic and vegetables and simmer for 10 minutes until just soft. Add in the dissolved cornflour to thicken and simmer for 2 minutes. Stir in the noodles and serve sprinkled with the sesame seeds.

# mushroom egg noodles

serves 2

100g medium egg noodles

3 tablespoons vegetable oil

3 garlic cloves, peeled and minced

3cm piece of ginger root, peeled
     and grated

200g mixed mushrooms (e.g.
     enoki, oyster, shiitake, button or
     field), trimmed and large ones
     torn in half

25g bamboo shoots, drained

125g tinned water chestnuts,
     rinsed, drained and halved
     if large

2 spring onions, cut into 3cm
     lengths

½ red pepper, deseeded and thinly
     sliced

2 tablespoons *tori kara age* sauce
     (see page 21)

salt and white pepper

2 handfuls of beansprouts

Cook the noodles according to the instructions on the packet, drain and refresh under cold water.

Heat 2 tablespoons of the oil in a hot wok over a high heat and stir fry the garlic and ginger for 30 seconds, then add all the mushrooms, bamboo shoots, water chestnuts, spring onions and red pepper. Stir fry for 2–3 minutes until the vegetables are just cooked, remove and set aside.

Wipe the wok clean and reheat. Add the remaining oil and stir fry the noodles for 1 minute. Add the *tori kara age* sauce and carry on cooking for 2 minutes. Return the mushroom mix and toss through to ensure that everything is heated through. Check the seasoning, top with the beansprouts and serve.

# wide noodle hot-pot with seven vegetables

serves 2

2 small pak choi, quartered
    lengthways
75g broccoli, cut into small florets
50g wide rice noodles
150ml chicken stock (see page 13)
2 tablespoons *mirin* (see page 11)
3 tablespoons soy sauce
2 teaspoons sugar
1 garlic clove, peeled and mashed
2cm piece of ginger root, peeled
    and grated
1 red chilli, chopped
handful of finely shredded Chinese
    cabbage
handful of mangetout
2 carrots, thinly sliced
1 small courgette, thinly sliced
4 shiitake mushrooms, thinly sliced
handful of coriander leaves

Blanch the pak choi and broccoli in a pan of boiling salted water until just tender. Drain and refresh under cold water.

Cook the noodles according to the instructions on the packet, drain and refresh under cold water.

Put the stock, *mirin,* soy sauce, sugar, garlic, ginger and chilli in a heavy, lidded saucepan, cover and bring to the boil. Add the Chinese cabbage, mangetout, carrots, courgette and mushrooms and cook for 4 minutes, or until softened but still crunchy. Add the blanched vegetables and noodles, check the seasoning and simmer over a gentle heat for 2 minutes. Allow to rest for 2 minutes, stir in the coriander and serve.

# aubergine hot-pot

serves 2

1 medium aubergine, trimmed and
    cut into 2cm dice
salt and white pepper
4 tablespoons vegetable oil
2 tablespoons finely chopped
    shallots
2 red chillies, chopped
3 garlic cloves, peeled and chopped
3cm piece of ginger root, peeled
    and finely chopped
3 lemongrass stalks, outer leaves
    removed, finely chopped
3 tablespoons *mirin* (see page 11)
500ml vegetable or chicken stock
    (see page 13)
100g *udon* noodles
4 handfuls of baby spinach
bunch of coriander, leaves picked

Sprinkle the aubergine with salt, place in a colander and set aside for 30 minutes. Rinse thoroughly in plenty of cold water and pat dry.

Heat 2 tablespoons of the oil in a hot wok and stir fry the aubergine for 5–6 minutes or until the pieces are golden brown. (You may need to do this in batches, if the wok is overcrowded everything will stew.) Remove and drain on kitchen paper.

Reheat the wok then add the remaining oil and stir fry the shallots, chilli, garlic, ginger and lemongrass for 3 minutes. Add the aubergine, *mirin* and stock and season with salt and pepper.

Reduce the heat and simmer for 10 minutes. Add the noodles and spinach and cook for 6–8 minutes or until the noodles are just tender and the liquid has thickened. Stir in the coriander, check the seasoning and serve.

200g raw, peeled tiger prawns
1 tablespoon lemon juice
1 teaspoon peeled and minced
    fresh ginger root
4 garlic cloves, peeled and mashed
200ml chicken stock (see
    page 13)
2 tablespoons *mirin* (see page 11)
2 tablespoons soy sauce
2 tablespoons chilli *ramen* sauce
    (see page 18)
2 teaspoons cornflour
100g *udon* noodles
2 tablespoons vegetable oil
1 small onion, thinly sliced
1 teaspoon hot chilli paste
generous handful of baby spinach
generous handful of beansprouts

# hot and sour prawn noodles

Toss the prawns with the lemon juice, ginger and half the garlic and set aside for 30 minutes. Combine the chicken stock, *mirin*, soy sauce, chilli *ramen* sauce and cornflour and set aside.

Cook the noodles according to the instructions on the packet, drain and rinse under cold water.

Heat a wok over a high heat, add 1 tablespoon of the oil and stir fry the prawns for 2 minutes, or until cooked. Remove and set aside.

Wipe the wok clean and reheat over a medium heat, adding the remaining oil. Stir fry the onion and remaining garlic with the chilli paste for 2 minutes until softened and just colouring. Add the chicken stock mixture and simmer for 3 minutes, stirring constantly.

When the sauce has thickened add the prawns, noodles and spinach. Mix gently for 1 minute to ensure everything is heated through, top with the beansprouts and serve.

100g *udon* noodles

2 tablespoons soy sauce

1 tablespoon *mirin* (see page 11)

2 teaspoons fish sauce (*nam pla*)

3cm piece of ginger root, peeled
    and grated

12 clams, well rinsed

100g shiitake mushrooms, cut into
    1cm strips

150g sea bass, cut into 3cm pieces

8 raw tiger prawns, peeled but tails
    on, and deveined

1 sheet of dried *nori* seaweed,
    cut into 1cm strips

100g tofu, cubed

1 head little gem lettuce, shredded

½ roll (100g) *kamaboko-aka* (see
    page 11), cut into 1cm slices

# seafood stew

Cook the noodles according to the instructions on the packet, drain and refresh under cold water.

Heat a heavy, lidded saucepan over a medium heat. Combine the soy sauce, *mirin*, fish sauce, and ginger with 200ml water and add to the pan. When the mixture is boiling add the clams. Put the lid on and steam for 2 minutes or until the shells start to open. Lift out the clams.

Add the mushrooms and sea bass, cover and cook for 2 minutes. Add the prawns and cook for a further 2 minutes with the lid on. Return the clams along with the seaweed, noodles, tofu and lettuce. Season with salt and pepper, cover and allow to sit for a further 3 minutes.

Serve with slices of *kamaboko-aka* scattered over.

serves 2

100g rice noodles

2 tablespoons vegetable oil

2 eggs, lightly beaten and seasoned

200g raw, peeled prawns

2 garlic cloves, peeled and finely
    chopped

1 chilli, deseeded and finely
    chopped

1 tablespoon fish sauce (*nam pla*)

1 tablespoon soy sauce

½ teaspoon soft brown sugar

handful of beansprouts

2 teaspoons dried shrimp, rinsed

2 spring onions, finely sliced

1 tablespoon chopped roasted
    peanuts

small bunch of coriander,
    leaves picked

1 lime, halved

# sweet and sour prawn noodles

Cook the noodles according to the instructions on the packet, drain and refresh under cold water.

Heat 1 tablespoon of the oil in a hot wok then add the egg, swirl around so that it thinly coats the bottom of the wok and cook until set, about 1 minute. Remove, allow to cool, then roll up and thinly slice.

Heat the remaining oil in the hot wok and stir fry the prawns, garlic and chilli for a scant 2 minutes, or until cooked. Add the fish sauce, soy sauce, sugar and noodles and stir fry for 1 minute. Add the beansprouts, dried shrimp, spring onions and reserved egg strips, toss well, and check the seasoning. Serve topped with the peanuts and coriander and the lime halves.

# spiced mussels with wide rice noodles

serves 2

150g wide rice noodles
1 tablespoon vegetable oil
1 onion, peeled and thinly sliced
3cm piece of ginger root, peeled
    and grated
3 garlic cloves, peeled and minced
1 green chilli, deseeded and finely
    chopped
½ teaspoon turmeric
2 star anise
large bunch of coriander, leaves
    picked, stems finely chopped
200ml coconut milk
500g mussels, scrubbed and
    debearded

Cook the noodles according to the instructions on the packet, drain and refresh under cold water.

Heat the vegetable oil in a hot wok and stir fry the onion for 2 minutes until softened and just catching colour. Add the ginger, garlic, chilli and turmeric and cook for a further minute, taking care not to let the mixture catch on the bottom.

Add the star anise and coriander stems and continue cooking for 30 seconds before adding the coconut milk. Bring to the boil, reduce the heat and allow to simmer for 1 minute so that everything thickens.

Add the mussels, turn up the heat and cover. Cook for 5 minutes or until the mussels start to open. Remove the cover, stir in the noodles and toss to ensure that everything is heated through and well coated.

Serve scattered with the reserved coriander leaves.

100g rice noodles

1 tablespoon vegetable oil

2 garlic cloves, peeled and finely minced

1 red onion, peeled and thinly sliced

1 small head broccoli, broken into florets

4 asparagus spears, trimmed

150g prepared squid, scored and cut into 3cm pieces

1 tablespoon soy sauce

1 teaspoon cornflour

200ml chicken stock (see page 13)

1 red chilli, finely sliced

# squid, broccoli and asparagus

Cook the noodles according to the instructions on the packet, drain and refresh under cold water. Toss with 1 teaspoon of the oil.

Heat the remaining oil in a hot wok and stir fry the garlic, red onion, broccoli, asparagus and squid for 4–5 minutes, or until they just start to colour. Combine the soy sauce and cornflour. Add the chicken stock and the cornflour mixture and simmer for 3 minutes. Add the noodles to the pan. Stir to ensure everything is well coated, and check the seasoning.

Serve with a scattering of the sliced chilli.

serves 2

100g rice noodles

2 tablespoons vegetable oil

2 eggs, beaten and seasoned

12 raw, peeled tiger prawns

6 shiitake mushrooms, sliced

6 spring onions, cut into 3cm lengths

2 garlic cloves, peeled and minced

50ml hoisin sauce

50ml chicken stock (see page 13)

50g spinach leaves

2 handfuls of beansprouts

# prawn, mushroom and spinach noodles

Cook the noodles according to the instructions on the packet, drain and refresh under cold water.

Heat 1 tablespoon of the oil in a hot wok then add the egg, swirl around so that it thinly coats the bottom of the wok and cook until set, about 1 minute. Remove, allow to cool, then roll up and thinly slice.

Heat the remaining oil in a hot wok, season the prawns and stir fry for 2–3 minutes. Add the mushrooms and spring onions and stir fry for 1 minute. Add the garlic and, 10 seconds later, the hoisin sauce and stock. Bring to the boil, cook for 1 minute and then add the spinach. Cook for a further 2 minutes or until the prawns are done.

Fold in the noodles and shredded egg, check the seasoning and serve topped with the beansprouts.

100g medium egg noodles

1 tablespoon vegetable oil

2 garlic cloves, peeled and roughly chopped

3cm piece of ginger root, peeled and grated

1 chilli, deseeded and finely sliced

200g raw, peeled prawns

bunch of coriander, leaves picked, stems finely chopped

salt and white pepper

1 tablespoon oyster sauce

1 tablespoon *mirin* (see page 11)

1 tablespoon fish sauce (*nam pla*)

10 water chestnuts, rinsed and drained

1 teaspoon toasted sesame oil

# spiced prawns with egg noodles and water chestnuts

Cook the noodles according to the instructions on the packet, drain and refresh under cold water. Toss with 1 teaspoon of the oil.

Heat the remaining oil in a hot wok and add the garlic. Sauté for 30 seconds then remove the garlic from the pan and reserve. Add the ginger, chilli, prawns and the coriander stems, season with salt and pepper and stir fry for 2–3 minutes or until the prawns are cooked.

Add the cooked noodles along with the oyster sauce, *mirin,* fish sauce, water chestnuts and sesame oil and simmer for 1 minute, stirring to combine and coat. Remove from the heat, stir in the reserved coriander leaves and check the seasoning. Serve scattered with the reserved garlic.

serves 2

100g rice vermicelli

1 tablespoon vegetable oil

75g prepared squid, cut into 3cm pieces

6 raw, unpeeled tiger prawns

salt and white pepper

200ml coconut milk

2 teaspoons dried shrimp, well rinsed

2 teaspoons fish sauce (*nam pla*)

1 tablespoon soy sauce

1 chilli, finely sliced

3cm piece of ginger root, peeled and grated

12 mussels, scrubbed and debearded

bunch of coriander, leaves picked

# thai-style seafood noodle curry

Cook the vermicelli according to the instructions on the packet, drain and refresh under cold water.

Heat the oil in a hot wok. Season the squid and prawns with salt and stir fry for 2–3 minutes or until cooked. Remove and set aside.

Add the coconut milk, dried shrimp, fish sauce, soy sauce, chilli and ginger to the wok and bring to the boil. Add the mussels and as soon as they start to open add the noodles. Stir well to ensure that everything is well combined, then add the reserved seafood. Toss gently, check the seasoning and serve scattered with the coriander leaves.

# salmon curry with rice noodles

serves 2

1 tablespoon vegetable oil

2 teaspoons finely chopped
    shallots

2 teaspoons red curry paste (see
    page 16)

125ml coconut milk

1 teaspoon muscovado sugar

2 teaspoons fish sauce (*nam pla*)

zest and juice of 1 lime,
    plus 1 lime, cut into wedges

2 skinless salmon fillets, each
    weighing about 100g

small handful of Thai basil leaves

small handful of mint leaves

100g wide rice noodles

Heat a sauté pan large enough to accommodate the salmon over a medium heat. Add the oil and shallots and cook until soft without colouring for 2 minutes.

Add the red curry paste and continue to cook for 2 minutes, stirring constantly. Add the coconut milk, sugar, fish sauce and the lime zest and juice. Bring to the boil, reduce to a gentle simmer for 5 minutes. taste and adjust the seasoning.

Ease the salmon fillets into the sauce and gently poach until the fish is cooked, about 8–10 minutes (depending on the thickness). Add the basil and mint.

Cook the noodles according to the instructions on the packet and drain immediately. Gently stir the noodles into the pot. Serve with the lime wedges on the side.

serves 2

for the marinade

2 teaspoons soy sauce

pinch of sugar

2 teaspoons *mirin* (see page 11)

2 teaspoons vegetable oil

salt and white pepper

200g salmon fillets, cutlets or tail
   end, cut into 2 pieces

100g *ramen* noodles

1 tablespoon vegetable oil

1 onion, peeled and finely sliced

1 small red pepper, deseeded and
   thinly sliced

3cm piece of ginger root, peeled
   and grated

2 garlic cloves, peeled and minced

1 tablespoon black bean sauce

1 red chilli, deseeded and finely
   sliced

250ml chicken stock (see
   page 13)

2 teaspoons cornflour, dissolved in
   2 tablespoons cold water

2 heads pak choi, trimmed and
   sliced very thinly lengthways

# marinated salmon, pak choi and black bean sauce

Combine the marinade ingredients in a medium bowl and season with salt and pepper. Add the salmon and turn to coat thoroughly. Set aside for at least 1 hour; overnight in the fridge is even better.

Cook the noodles according to the instructions on the packet, drain and refresh under cold water.

Preheat the grill to high. Remove the salmon pieces (reserve the marinade) and cook the salmon for 5 minutes, or until cooked through, turning once.

Heat the vegetable oil in a hot wok and stir fry the onion, red pepper, ginger and garlic for 1 minute. Add the black bean sauce, chilli, chicken stock, reserved marinade and dissolved cornflour and simmer for 2 minutes. Stir in the noodles and pak choi and cook for a further minute until the pak choi has wilted.

Top with the salmon and serve.

for the marinade
3cm piece of ginger root, peeled
    and grated
3 garlic cloves, peeled and grated
1 tablespoon *mirin* (see page 11)
2 teaspoons fish sauce (*nam pla*)

200g monkfish fillet, cut into
    1cm discs
100g thin egg noodles
200g broccoli, cut into florets
1 tablespoon vegetable oil
2 tablespoons oyster sauce
4 spring onions, finely sliced
1 red chilli, finely sliced
2 teaspoons sesame seeds, briefly
    toasted in a hot, dry frying pan
2 teaspoons toasted sesame oil

# marinated monkfish with broccoli and oyster sauce

Combine the marinade ingredients in a medium bowl. Add the monkfish to the marinade and turn to coat thoroughly. Set aside for a few hours in the fridge; overnight is even better.

Cook the noodles according to the instructions on the packet, drain and refresh under cold water. Blanch the broccoli in boiling salted water until just tender, drain and refresh under cold water.

Heat the vegetable oil in a hot wok and stir fry the monkfish for 2 minutes. Add the broccoli and stir fry for 1 minute. Add the oyster sauce, check the seasoning, then stir in the drained noodles.

Serve scattered with the spring onions, chilli, sesame seeds and a drizzle of sesame oil.

serves 2

100g *somen* noodles
200g spinach
3cm piece of ginger root, peeled
    and grated
1 tablespoon soy sauce
2 garlic cloves, peeled and
    thinly sliced
juice of 1 lemon
1 teaspoon fish sauce (*nam pla*)
1 teaspoon rice vinegar
1 tablespoon vegetable oil
4 spring onions, cut into 3cm lengths
2 teaspoons cornflour, seasoned
    with salt and white pepper
200g sea bass fillets, cut into
    bite-sized pieces
2 teaspoons toasted sesame oil
1 teaspoon sesame seeds, briefly
    toasted in a hot, dry frying pan

# stir-fried sea bass with spinach and spring onions

Cook the noodles according to the instructions on the packet, drain and refresh under cold water.

Blanch the spinach in boiling salted water for 30 seconds or until just wilted. Drain and refresh under cold water and squeeze gently. Fluff up the spinach and set aside.

Combine the ginger, soy sauce, garlic, lemon juice, fish sauce and rice vinegar in a bowl. Heat the oil in a hot wok and stir fry the spring onions for 1 minute or until they just start to colour.

Dust the sea bass with the seasoned cornflour. Add to the pan and stir fry for 2–3 minutes or until the fish is almost cooked. Add the spinach, noodles and the ginger mixture and cook until everything is amalgamated and bubbling. Remove from the heat, pour over the sesame oil and serve scattered with the sesame seeds.

# peppered mackerel with ramen noodles

serves 2

½ teaspoon szechwan peppercorns
½ teaspoon black peppercorns
200g *ramen* noodles
1 tablespoon vegetable oil
2 small red onions, peeled and cut
    vertically into eighths
2 teaspoons oyster sauce
2 teaspoons hoisin sauce
1 teaspoon cornflour, dissolved in
    2 tablespoons water
juice of 1 lime
150g skinless mackerel fillet, cut
    into bite-sized pieces
handful of beansprouts

Heat a dry frying pan and toast the peppercorns together until they release their aromas. Transfer to a pestle and mortar and crush.

Cook the noodles according to the instructions on the packet, drain and refresh under cold water.

Heat the vegetable oil in a hot wok and stir fry the crushed peppercorns and red onions for 4 minutes until the onions start to colour.

Combine the oyster sauce, hoisin sauce, cornflour and lime juice. Add this mixture and the mackerel to the wok and stir fry for 2 minutes until the fish is cooked. Add the noodles, toss well to ensure everything is well coated.

Serve topped with the beansprouts.

# prawn and chicken noodles

serves 2

100g medium egg noodles
1 tablespoon vegetable oil
1 tablespoon shallots, peeled and
    cut into half-moon slices
3cm piece of ginger root, peeled
    and finely chopped
2 garlic cloves, peeled and chopped
100g minced chicken
100g raw, peeled prawns
handful of finely sliced Chinese
    cabbage
100g water chestnuts, chopped
1 egg, lightly beaten and seasoned
1 tablespoon curry powder
2 tablespoons soy sauce
1 tablespoon *mirin* (see page 11)
1 teaspoon sugar
handful of beansprouts
2 tablespoons oyster sauce
2 teaspoons toasted sesame oil
2 spring onions, finely sliced

Cook the noodles according to the instructions on the packet, drain and refresh under cold water.

Heat the oil in a hot wok and stir fry the shallots, ginger and garlic for 1 minute. Add the chicken, prawns, Chinese cabbage and water chestnuts and stir fry for 2 minutes. Add the egg, stirring it into the other ingredients for about 30 seconds.

Add the curry powder, soy sauce, *mirin* and sugar along with the noodles and beansprouts and toss everything to heat through for 1 minute. Remove from the heat and stir in the oyster sauce and sesame oil.

Serve topped with the spring onions.

**serves 2**

3 tablespoons vegetable oil

150g boneless, skinless chicken
    breast, diced

1 courgette, diced

½ small aubergine, diced

2 spring onions, cut into 1cm
    pieces

1 garlic clove, peeled and finely
    chopped

3cm piece of ginger root, peeled
    and finely chopped

1 tablespoon green curry paste
    (see page 18)

250ml chicken stock (see
    page 13)

175ml coconut milk

1 tablespoon fish sauce (*nam pla*)

100g medium egg noodles

juice of 1 lime

2 tablespoons roughly chopped
    coriander

2 tablespoons unsalted peanuts

Heat 1 tablespoon of the vegetable oil in a hot wok over a medium heat and stir fry the chicken for 3–4 minutes, or until golden brown. Remove and set aside.

Add the remaining oil to the wok and stir fry the courgette and aubergine for 4 minutes, or until golden brown. The aubergine tends to soak up the oil at first and then release it.

Add the spring onions, stir fry for 1 minute and then add the garlic and ginger. Cook for 1 minute and then stir in the curry paste.

Pour in the chicken stock, coconut milk and fish sauce, bring to the boil and simmer for 10 minutes. Add the noodles and reserved chicken and cook for about 4 minutes or until the noodles are tender. Add the lime juice and check the seasoning.

Serve sprinkled with the coriander and peanuts.

## stir-fried prawns and pork with crispy noodles

serves 2

100g raw, peeled tiger prawns
50g rice vermicelli
vegetable oil
2 tablespoons finely chopped
    shallots
3 garlic cloves, peeled and finely
    sliced
pinch of chilli flakes (or to taste)
200g minced pork
large handful of beansprouts
½ teaspoon light brown sugar
1 tablespoon fish sauce (nam pla)
1 tablespoon mirin (see page 11)
small handful of coriander leaves
juice of 1 lime

Butterfly the prawns by cutting each one lengthways almost right the way through, and open out the two halves.

Put the vermicelli into a small bag and break into short lengths. Heat 3cm of oil in a wok to 180°C (drop in a piece of vermicelli: it will puff up if the oil is hot enough). Cook the noodles in batches: they puff up immediately so you need to extract them quickly. Drain on kitchen paper as they are cooked.

Heat 1 tablespoon oil in a hot wok and stir fry the shallots for 1 minute. Add the garlic, chilli flakes and pork and continue stir frying for a further 2 minutes or until the pork is almost cooked. Add the prawns, beansprouts, sugar, fish sauce and mirin and continue stir frying for a further 2–3 minutes or until the prawns are cooked. Toss the coriander through.

Serve the pork and prawn mixture on top of the noodles with the lime juice squeezed over.

## pork, prawn, rice and noodle hot-pot

serves 2

100g pork fillet, thinly sliced
2 garlic cloves, peeled and crushed
2 tablespoons soy sauce
75g basmati rice
4 small dried shiitake mushrooms
1 tablespoon vegetable oil
100g raw, peeled tiger prawns,
    deveined
500ml chicken stock (see
    page 13)
1 tablespoon fish sauce (nam pla)
75g medium egg noodles, broken
    into 4cm lengths
2 pak choi, quartered lengthways
1 lime, cut into wedges

Combine the pork, garlic and soy sauce in a bowl and set aside.

Rinse the rice in plenty of cold water and leave to stand, covered by a good few centimetres of water for 30 minutes, or an hour if possible.

Place the mushrooms in a bowl, pour boiling water over them and set aside for 20 minutes or until soft. Slice the mushrooms, reserving the liquid.

Heat the oil in a hot wok and sauté the pork, garlic and soy sauce for 1 minute. Stir in the prawns, mushrooms and mushroom liquid, and sauté for a further minute. Add the stock and fish sauce. Bring to the boil, add the rice and cook gently for about 5 minutes then add the noodles and pak choi and continue cooking for a further 4 minutes or until both the rice and noodles are cooked.

Check the seasoning and serve with the lime wedges.

*If you don't soak the rice it takes much longer to cook which makes adding the noodles at the right time difficult.*

# stir-fried pork noodles

serves 2

**for the marinade**

1 garlic clove, peeled and chopped
   then crushed with a little salt
3cm piece of ginger root, peeled
   and grated
1 tablespoon soy sauce

100g pork fillet, cut into thin strips
150g rice vermicelli
1 tablespoon dried shrimp, well
   rinsed
handful of French beans, trimmed
1 tablespoon vegetable oil
50g button mushrooms, finely sliced
2 handfuls of spinach
soy sauce
2 spring onions, finely sliced

Combine the marinade ingredients in a medium bowl. Add the pork, toss well and set aside for 1 hour or so; overnight in the fridge is even better.

Cook the vermicelli according to the instructions on the packet, drain and refesh under cold water.

Soak the shrimp in boiling water for 10 minutes, strain, reserving the liquid. Cook the beans in salted water until just tender but with some bite, drain and refresh under cold water.

Heat the oil in a hot wok and stir fry the mushroooms, pork and its marinade for 3 minutes. Add the beans and spinach and stir fry for 1 minute until wilted. Add the vermicelli, reserved shrimp liquid and season with soy sauce to taste.

Serve with the reserved shrimps and spring onions scattered over the top.

# marinated pork and cellophane noodles

serves 2

**for the marinade**

1 tablespoon soy sauce
1 tablespoon *mirin* (see page 11)
1 teaspoon chilli oil
2 teaspoons peeled and grated
   fresh ginger root
2 garlic cloves, peeled and crushed

200g pork fillet or tenderloin,
   trimmed and sliced
75g cellophane noodles
2 tablespoons vegetable oil
4 spring onions, cut into 3cm
   pieces
2 pak choi, roughly chopped
small bunch of coriander, roughly
   chopped
1 teaspoon cornflour
100ml chicken stock (see page 13)
salt and white pepper

Combine the marinade ingredients in a medium bowl and add the pork. Stir to combine well and leave for 30 minutes; overnight in the fridge is even better. Drain and reserve the excess marinade.

Cook the noodles according to the instructions on the packet, drain and refresh under cold water.

Heat the oil in a hot wok then add the pork. Stir fry to seal for 2 minutes. Add the spring onions, pak choi and coriander and stir fry for a further minute.

Mix the cornflour with a little of the chicken stock. Add this to the wok with the remaining stock and the reserved marinade, and cook for 1 minute. Add the noodles and continue cooking until everything is thick and syrupy. Taste and adjust the seasoning before serving.

serves 2

## for the marinade

3cm piece of ginger root, peeled
    and grated
2 garlic cloves, peeled and finely
    chopped or grated
1 tablespoon soy sauce

100g pork loin, trimmed and cut
    into strips
salt and white pepper
150g rice noodles
2 tablespoons vegetable oil
60g tofu, in one piece
30g unsalted peanuts
1 garlic clove, peeled and crushed
1 small red onion, peeled and
    thinly sliced
1 green chilli, deseeded and
    thinly sliced
100g beansprouts
60g Chinese flowering chives
    (see page 11), finely sliced
1 tablespoon dark soy sauce
coriander leaves

# marinated pork and tofu with rice noodles

Combine the marinade ingredients in a medium bowl. Add the pork, mix thoroughly, season and leave for 1 hour; overnight in the fridge is even better.

Cook the noodles according to the instructions on the packet, drain and refresh under cold water.

Heat 1 tablespoon of the oil in a hot wok, season the tofu and fry for 2 minutes, turning until golden brown all over. Remove and allow to cool. Add the peanuts to the hot oil and stir fry for 30 seconds until golden brown, then set aside to drain on a few sheets of kitchen paper.

Wipe the wok clean with kitchen paper, reheat, then add the remaining oil. Drain and reserve the marinade from the pork. Add the garlic to the wok and stir fry for a few seconds. Add the meat and stir fry for 1 minute to seal. Add the onion to the wok and continue cooking for 2–3 minutes until soft and just beginning to colour. Add the chilli and stir fry for 30 seconds. Add the noodles, beansprouts, Chinese chives and half the peanuts. Add the dark soy sauce and reserved marinade and continue cooking for a further 3 minutes.

Thinly slice the tofu into four and add, tossing gently so the tofu doesn't break up too much. Serve scattered with the remaining peanuts and the coriander leaves.

100g rice vermicelli

3 tablespoons vegetable oil

2 teaspoons finely chopped
    shallots

1 garlic clove, peeled and thinly
    sliced

1cm piece of ginger root, peeled
    and finely chopped

40g pork, julienned

pinch of dried red chilli flakes

2 shiitake mushrooms, sliced

1 tablespoon soy sauce

75g raw, peeled prawns, deveined
    and halved lengthways

½ teaspoon sugar

1 egg, lightly beaten

50g beansprouts

50g tinned chestnuts, drained,
    rinsed and roughly chopped

2 spring onions, green parts
    included, finely sliced

coriander leaves

# pork, prawn and mushroom noodles

Cook the vermicelli according to the instructions on the packet, drain and refresh under cold water.

Heat the oil in a hot wok. When almost smoking add the shallots, garlic and ginger and stir fry for 1 minute, then add the pork, chilli flakes and mushrooms. Stir fry for a further 2 minutes and add the soy sauce. Add the prawns and stir fry for a further minute.

Add 2 tablespoons water, the sugar and the egg. Stir fry so the egg just cooks and remove from the heat. Add in the noodles, beansprouts, and chestnuts and top with the spring onions and coriander.

# spiced beef noodles

200g *udon* noodles
200g beef sirloin or rump, cut into
    strips 5mm thick
1 tablespoon cornflour
salt and white pepper
2 tablespoons vegetable oil
3cm piece of ginger root, peeled
    and grated
4 handfuls of baby spinach
2 spring onions, cut into
    4cm lengths
1 tablespoon soy sauce
1 red chilli, deseeded and
    finely sliced
2 teaspoons toasted sesame oil
1 teaspoon sesame seeds, briefly
    toasted in a hot, dry frying pan

Cook the noodles according to the instructions on the packet, drain and refresh under cold water.

Put the beef, cornflour and salt and pepper in a plastic bag and toss the meat to coat. Set aside.

Heat the oil in a hot wok, add the ginger and cook for 30 seconds. Add the beef and stir fry for 2 minutes, or until the beef is just cooked.

Add the spinach, spring onions and 1 tablespoon water and toss for 1 minute so everything is just wilted. Add the soy sauce and chilli. Taste and adjust the seasoning. Add the noodles, toss to ensure that everything is combined and top with the toasted sesame oil and sesame seeds.

# hot and sour beef ramen

serve 2

75g *ramen* noodles

150g beef fillet

2 garlic cloves, peeled and minced

1 red chilli, thinly sliced

1 tablespoon rice vinegar

1 tablespoon soy sauce

650ml chicken stock (see page 13)
    or beef stock

½ small red onion, peeled and
    thinly sliced

2 handfuls of beansprouts

2 teaspoons toasted sesame oil

1 teaspoon sesame seeds, briefly
    toasted in a hot, dry frying pan

Cook the noodles according to the instructions on the packet, drain and refresh under cold water. Slice the beef as thinly as possible.

Put the garlic, chilli, rice vinegar and soy sauce with the stock in a large pan. Bring to the boil, simmer for 2 minutes, then add the beef and cook for a scant minute.

Add the noodles and swirl everything about. Top with the red onion, beansprouts and toasted sesame oil and seeds, and serve.

# stir-fried chilli beef with broccoli

serves 2

**for the marinade**

1 red chilli, deseeded and sliced

3cm piece of ginger root, peeled
    and grated

1 garlic clove, peeled and sliced

½ teaspoon sugar

zest and juice of 1 lime

2 teaspoons cornflour

1 tablespoon vegetable oil

200g rump steak, trimmed of any
    fat and cut into thin strips

100g medium egg noodles

150g broccoli, broken into small
    florets

2 tablespoons vegetable oil

1 tablespoon finely sliced shallots

1 tablespoon *mirin* (see page 11)

1 teaspoon fish sauce (*nam pla*)

salt and pepper

soy sauce

½ teaspoon sesame seeds, briefly
    toasted in a hot, dry frying pan

Combine the marinade ingredients in a medium bowl. Add the steak, toss well to combine, and set aside for at least 1 hour; overnight in the fridge is even better.

Cook the noodles according to the instructions on the packet, drain and refresh under cold water.

Blanch the broccoli in boiling salted water for 2–3 minutes or until just cooked. Drain and refresh under cold water.

Heat the oil in a hot wok over a high heat and stir fry the shallots until they just start to colour, about 30 seconds. Add the beef and its marinade and continue to cook for a further 2 minutes. Add the noodles, broccoli, *mirin*, fish sauce and 1 tablespoon soy sauce and continue to stir fry for a further 2 minutes or until the meat is cooked and everything is heated through. Season to taste with salt and pepper and soy sauce.

Sprinkle with the sesame seeds and serve.

# children

Children love noodles. They are so easygoing (the noodles that is). You can eat, slurp and suck, use chopsticks, fingers or a fork. The noodles don't mind and nor do the children. As adults these things seem to matter – sort of. But children see beyond that. It is a good partnership.

Noodles are not fussy, they just know what they like. A similarity there from the start. Children get on with things and noodles like that. There is an honesty, an immediacy, which is refreshing. Why make a big fuss over something when there is no need to? What is a noodle other than food? And rather a nice one at that.

The recipes in this chapter tend to be short and stick to easy ingredients, the kind that children tell us they like. This makes them easy to cook, so if the occasion, allows your children can join in too. It is bonding of the best kind. Getting to know your food is, after all, a sure way of feeling involved. Which makes saying yes, or yum for that matter, so much easier.

Short ingredient lists still mean the rather more complex tastes of soy sauce and ginger, garlic and sesame can come into play. Perhaps in muted form. The idea is to encourage exploration. A sense of adventure.

We've tried to keep things simple in this chapter. A kind of introduction. On the basis that enthusiasm and experience is likely to lead to a sense of adventure when other chapters can play a role. After all, children never stay the same. At least that is what we have found.

serves 2

for the dressing

2 tablespoons *mirin* (see page 11)

2 tablespoons rice vinegar

2 tablespoons oyster sauce

1 tablespoon sweet chilli sauce

1 garlic clove, peeled and minced

3cm piece of ginger root, peeled
    and grated

100g rice vermicelli

small handful of mangetout

1 tablespoon fresh peas, cooked

½ red pepper, deseeded and cut
    into short, fine slices

1 small courgette, thinly sliced

4 radishes, thinly sliced

handful of baby spinach leaves

salt and white pepper

2 teaspoons sesame seeds, briefly
    toasted in a hot, dry frying pan

# spring salad with toasted sesame seeds

Cook the vermicelli according to the instructions on the packet, drain and refresh briefly under cold water. Roughly chop.

Combine the dressing ingredients in a large bowl and toss the warm vermicelli through.

Add the mangetout, peas, red pepper, courgette, radishes and spinach to the noodles and toss to ensure that everything is well combined. Taste and season with salt and pepper.

Serve sprinkled with the sesame seeds.

serves 2

150g thin white *somen* noodles

1 tablespoon vegetable oil

1 red onion, peeled and thinly sliced

1 red pepper, deseeded and sliced

½ Chinese cabbage, thinly sliced

8 button mushrooms, thinly sliced

1 tablespoon *kare lomen* sauce
    (see page 21)

1 tablespoon soy sauce

salt and white pepper

½ teaspoon sugar

½ teaspoon *dashi no moto*
    (see page 11)

handful of beansprouts

bunch of coriander, leaves picked

¼ cucumber, deseeded and
    julienned

# lightly curried vegetable noodles

Cook the noodles according to the instructions on the packet, drain and refresh under cold water.

Heat the vegetable oil in a hot wok over a medium–high heat and stir fry the red onion, red pepper, cabbage and mushrooms for 2 minutes. Add the *kare lomen* sauce and stir fry for 5 minutes until the mixture starts to colour and the aroma becomes sweet and rounded. Add the soy sauce, 150ml water, season with salt and pepper, add the sugar and *dashi no moto* and simmer for 1 minute.

Divide the noodles between 2 bowls and spoon over the vegetables. Serve topped with the beansprouts, coriander and cucumber.

100g wide rice noodles
1 tablespoon vegetable oil
1 garlic clove, peeled and finely
  chopped
2 lemongrass stalks, outer leaves
  removed, finely chopped
1 egg, beaten and seasoned
150g raw, peeled prawns
1 tablespoon fish sauce (*nam pla*)
1 teaspoon soft brown sugar
2 teaspoons soy sauce
large handful of roasted peanuts,
  coarsely chopped
handful of beansprouts
small bunch of coriander, leaves
  picked

# thai-style prawns and fried noodles

Cook the noodles according to the instructions on the packet, drain and refresh under cold water.

Heat the oil in a hot wok and stir fry the garlic and lemongrass for 30 seconds. Add the egg, swirl it around for 30 seconds, then add the noodles, prawns, fish sauce, sugar, soy sauce and half the peanuts. Stir fry to cook the prawns, about 2 minutes.

Add the beansprouts and coriander, check the seasoning and toss for 1 minute to ensure that everything is heated through.

Serve with the remaining peanuts scattered over the top.

serves 4 small ones

150g thin egg noodles
1 tablespoon vegetable oil
1 garlic clove, peeled and finely
  chopped
1cm piece of ginger root, peeled
  and finely chopped
150g raw, peeled prawns
3 tablespoons frozen peas,
  defrosted
1 tablespoon soy sauce
1 teaspoon cornflour, dissolved in
  2 tablespoons water
150ml chicken stock (see
  page 13)
salt and white pepper

# stir-fried prawns and peas

Cook the noodles according to the instructions on the packet, drain and refresh under cold water.

Heat the oil in a hot wok and add the garlic and ginger, toss and then add the prawns and stir fry for 1 minute. Add the peas, cook for a further minute, then add the noodles, soy sauce, dissolved cornflour and chicken stock. Season with salt and pepper and cook to ensure that everything is heated through, and serve.

125g medium egg noodles

2 teaspoons vegetable oil

1 tablespoon red curry paste
    (see page 16)

1 tablespoon coconut milk

juice of 1 lime

2 teaspoons fish sauce (*nam pla*)

2 teaspoons finely chopped
    shallots

500g mussels, scrubbed and
    debearded

handful of spinach leaves

# thai-style mussels with egg noodles

Cook the noodles according to the instructions on the packet, drain and refresh under cold water.

Heat the oil in a hot wok with a lid (or a large lidded saucepan) and stir fry the curry paste, coconut milk, lime juice, fish sauce and shallots for 3 minutes, ensuring the mixture doesn't catch. You want the curry paste to lose its raw aroma.

Add the mussels and toss so that everything is well combined. Cover, reduce the heat and cook for 5 minutes, shaking the pan occasionally, until all the mussels open. Discard any mussels that remain closed.

Remove the lid, stir in the drained noodles and spinach and check the seasoning. Cook for 1 minute, until the noodles are heated through and the spinach just wilted. Serve.

100g medium egg noodles

1 tablespoon vegetable oil

1 garlic clove, peeled and finely
    chopped

100g chicken thigh meat, cut into
    bite-sized pieces

handful of mangetout, thinly sliced
    lengthways

1 tablespoon soy sauce

2 teaspoons fish sauce (*nam pla*)

165g tinned sweetcorn, drained
    weight

salt and white pepper

2 teaspoons sesame seeds, briefly
    toasted in a hot, dry frying pan

1 teaspoon toasted sesame oil

bunch of coriander, leaves picked

# stir-fried chicken and sweetcorn

Cook the noodles according to the instructions on the packet, drain and refresh under cold water.

Heat the oil in a hot wok and stir fry the garlic for 30 seconds. Add the chicken, and continue to stir fry for 3–4 minutes or until the meat is cooked. Add the mangetout, soy sauce and fish sauce and simmer for 30 seconds before adding the noodles and sweetcorn. Season with salt and pepper and continue to cook for 1 minute.

Remove from the heat, add the sesame seeds and sesame oil and toss to coat everything well.

Serve scattered with the coriander.

# beef and orange stir fry

serves 4 small ones

100g wide rice noodles
1 tablespoon vegetable oil
1 garlic clove, peeled and finely
    chopped
3cm piece of ginger root, peeled
    and grated
200g sirloin steak, cut into thin strips
1 medium carrot, julienned
handful of mangetout, sliced thinly
    lengthways
zest and juice of 1 orange
1 tablespoon soy sauce
2 teaspoons oyster sauce
1 tablespoon toasted sesame oil
handful of beansprouts
1 tablespoon sesame seeds, briefly
    toasted in a hot, dry frying pan

Cook the noodles according to the instructions on the packet, drain and refresh under cold water.

Heat the oil in a hot wok, and stir fry the garlic and ginger for 30 seconds. Add the beef and carrot and stir fry for 3 minutes. Add the mangetout and continue to stir fry for 1 minute. Add the orange zest and juice, soy sauce, oyster sauce, sesame oil and beansprouts. Add the noodles and toss to ensure that everything is well coated and heated through. Check the seasoning.

Serve with a scattering of sesame seeds.

# marinated chicken with orange, soy sauce and ginger

serves 4 small ones

for the marinade
3cm piece of ginger root, peeled
    and grated
1 garlic clove, peeled and minced
zest and juice of 1 orange
1 tablespoon soy sauce
1 tablespoon muscovado sugar

200g boneless dark chicken meat
    (leg or thigh), roughly chopped
150g medium egg noodles
1 tablespoon vegetable oil
handful of mangetout, thinly sliced
75g baby corn, halved lengthways
100ml chicken stock (see page 13)
1 tablespoon cornflour
1 tablespoon toasted sesame oil
1 tablespoon sesame seeds, briefly
    toasted in a hot, dry frying pan
1 lime, quartered

Combine the marinade ingredients in a small pan and gently heat to dissolve the sugar. Allow to cool and add the chicken, toss so that it is well coated and set aside for at least 1 hour; overnight in the fridge is even better.

Cook the noodles according to the instructions on the packet, drain and refresh under cold water.

Heat the oil in a hot wok, add the chicken (reserve the marinade), and stir fry for 2–3 minutes until golden. Add the mangetout, baby corn, reserved marinade and chicken stock and continue to stir fry for 2 minutes, or until the chicken is cooked and the vegetables are just wilting. Dissolve the cornflour in 1 tablespoon water, add to the wok and simmer for 1 minute until thickened.

Add the noodles and toss through, along with the sesame oil, to ensure everything is well coated and heated through.

Serve scattered with the sesame seeds and with a lime wedge.

# salads

Cold noodles? What a thought. Yet this is common throughout Asia and has been for centuries. A Sunday treat in Japan is ice-cold buckwheat noodles and soy dipping sauce. Surprisingly good.

This chapter is full of cold noodles. Dressed, along with other ingredients, is a pretty good definition of a salad. On a hot day what can be more yummy than the chilled tingle of ginger and soy with crunchy vegetables. Refreshing too. The same is true of fish. Think of an Italian seafood salad with potatoes and you get the idea. Only with noodles you get added slurp.

A salad is a good contrast in any assembly of dishes. Some might say a little light relief. We like to think of noodle salads as rather more important than that. A difference with attitude. The noodles that bring flavour – like *somen* – are quite a surprise really. Chilling a noodle does rather a lot for its character. Sort of draws it out. So what might add crunch – as beanthreads do – reveals rather a clean delicate flavour when eaten cold. All the other noodles, wheat and rice, come across with surprising flavour profiles. But then, served cold, so do quite a lot of other ingredients. Lettuce for instance. And peas. And all this is before you consider your dressing. And seasoning.

Your dressing is what brings everything together. It must perform however. *Nam pla* (fish sauce) might seem an odd ingredient to put in a dressing but its sourness works wonders. Lime juice adds acidity. Soy an unmistakeable zest. Sesame oil brings a rich nuttiness. Sugar a sweetness. Combined and in the right proportion you have a kind of happiness. The kind you want to eat.

# spinach and potato noodle salad

serves 2

1 medium potato, peeled and cut
 into 3cm cubes
100g cellophane noodles
2 tablespoons vegetable oil
1 tablespoon finely chopped shallots
½ teaspoon turmeric
1 tablespoon fish sauce (*nam pla*)
1 tablespoon toasted sesame oil
2 handfuls of baby spinach leaves
zest and juice of 1 lemon
salt and white pepper

Put the potatoes in cold, salted water, bring to the boil and simmer for about 8 minutes, or until tender.

Soften the noodles according to the instructions on the packet, drain and refresh under cold water.

Heat the oil in a hot wok and stir fry the shallots and turmeric for 1–2 minutes, or until golden brown. Add the fish sauce, remove from the heat and stir in the noodles and sesame oil. Transfer to a bowl.

Drain the potatoes and toss through gently to ensure that everything is heated through. Add the spinach, lemon zest and juice, toss again, check the seasoning and serve.

# rice noodle salad

serves 2

50g medium rice noodles
25g frozen peas
2 spring onions, finely sliced
6 radishes, finely sliced
5cm cucumber, cut into half-moon
 slices
small handful of beansprouts
1 red chilli (or to taste),
 deseeded and finely sliced
small handful of mangetout,
 finely sliced
2 teaspoons fish sauce (*nam pla*)
1 teaspoon soft brown sugar
1 teaspoon soy sauce
zest and juice of 1 lime
1cm piece of ginger root, peeled
 and grated
1 garlic clove, peeled and
 finely sliced
toasted sesame oil
salt and white pepper
2 tablespoons chopped coriander
2 teaspoons roughly chopped
 roasted peanuts

Cook the noodles according to the instructions on the packet, drain and refresh under cold water.

Cook the peas for 1 minute in boiling unsalted water, then plunge into cold water. When cold, toss with the other prepared vegetables and the noodles.

Combine the fish sauce, sugar and soy sauce in a small pan and heat until the sugar just dissolves. Add the lime zest and juice, ginger and garlic and 1 tablespoon sesame oil. Pour over the noodle mixture, toss well, season with salt and pepper and add more sesame oil to taste.

Serve scattered with the coriander leaves and peanuts.

# soba noodle salad

serves 2

for the dressing
1 teaspoon honey
1 teaspoon fish sauce (*nam pla*)
1 teaspoon rice vinegar
1 teaspoon *mirin* (see page 11)

100g *soba* noodles
zest and juice of 1 lime
8 radishes, thinly sliced
½ cucumber, deseeded and
    finely sliced
1 carrot, julienned
bunch of mint, leaves roughly chopped
2 handfuls of spinach, roughly
    chopped
salt and white pepper

Cook the noodles according to the instructions on the packet, drain and refresh under cold water.

Mix together the dressing ingredients in a small pan, bring to the boil and set aside to cool. Stir in the lime zest and juice.

Combine the noodles with the radishes, cucumber, carrot, mint and spinach, add the cooled dressing and toss to ensure that everything is coated. Check the seasoning and serve.

# summer salad with pickled ginger

serves 2

100g rice vermicelli
bunch of asparagus spears, woody
    ends removed
1 tablespoon vegetable oil
2 eggs, beaten and seasoned
½ cucumber, julienned
1 medium carrot, julienned
handful of beansprouts
1 red chilli, deseeded and sliced
handful of mint leaves
1 sheet of *nori* seaweed,
    roughly torn
1 teaspoon sesame seeds

for the dressing
2 teaspoons soy sauce
2 teaspoons pickled ginger, roughly
    chopped
1 teaspoon fish sauce (*nam pla*)
2 teaspoons *mirin* (see page 11)
juice of 1 lime

Cook the vermicelli according to the instructions on the packet, drain and refresh in cold water. Roughly chop.

Cook the asparagus in boiling salted water for 3–5 minutes (depending on thickness) until just tender. Drain and refresh in cold water and cut in half.

Heat the oil in a hot wok then add the egg, swirl around so that it thinly coats the bottom of the wok and cook until set, about 1 minute. Remove, allow to cool, then roll up and thinly slice.

Combine the egg, noodles and asparagus with the cucumber, carrot, beansprouts and chilli.

Mix together the dressing ingredients and add to the salad.

Transfer to a plate and serve scattered with the mint leaves, *nori* and sesame seeds.

# pickled vegetable noodles

serves 2

2 teaspoons *mirin* (see page 11)
2 teaspoons soy sauce
2 teaspoons toasted sesame oil
pinch of sugar
1 garlic clove, peeled and crushed
100g *kimchee* (see page 11),
    roughly chopped, juices
    reserved
1 cucumber, shaved into long thin
    strips with a vegetable peeler
1 red onion, peeled and thinly
    sliced
2 carrots, julienned
150g *somen* noodles
1 teaspoon sesame seeds, briefly
    toasted in a hot, dry frying pan
2 teaspoons roughly chopped
    roasted peanuts

Combine the *mirin*, soy sauce, sesame oil and sugar with the garlic and stir in the *kimchee*. Add the cucumber, red onion and carrots. Toss gently to coat everything with dressing and set aside.

Cook the noodles according to the instructions on the packet, drain and refresh under cold water.

Add the noodles, sesame seeds and reserved *kimchee* juices to the salad and toss to ensure that everything is well coated.

Serve topped with the chopped peanuts.

# mushroom salad with somen noodles

serves 2

100g button mushrooms, quartered
1 tablespoon rice vinegar
2 garlic cloves, peeled and minced
bunch of coriander, leaves picked,
    stems finely chopped
2 tablespoons vegetable oil
1 tablespoon toasted sesame oil
75g *somen* noodles
1 tablespoon soy sauce
1 tablespoon sweet dipping chilli
    sauce (see page 16)
4 spring onions, finely sliced
2 heads little gem lettuce, finely
    sliced
1 carrot, peeled and cut into
    matchsticks
bunch of mint, roughly chopped
1 lime, halved

Combine the mushrooms with the rice vinegar, garlic, coriander stems, vegetable oil, sesame oil and 2 tablespoons water in a saucepan. Cover and simmer, stirring occasionally for 8–10 minutes or until the mushrooms have wilted but retain some bite. Leave to cool.

Cook the noodles according to the instructions on the packet, drain and refresh under cold water.

Combine the noodles with the soy sauce, sweet chilli sauce, spring onions, lettuce, carrot, mint and reserved coriander leaves. Add the mushrooms and their juices and toss to ensure that everything is well coated.

Serve with the lime halves.

1 teaspoon soft light brown sugar
2 teaspoons fish sauce (*nam pla*)
juice of 1 lime
1 tablespoon vegetable oil
12 cooked, peeled prawns
100g cellophane noodles
6 asparagus spears, cut into
    4cm lengths
¼ cucumber, deseeded and
    julienned
6 radishes, finely sliced
1 red chilli (or to taste), deseeded
    and finely chopped
1 garlic clove, peeled and finely
    chopped
2 spring onions, finely sliced
small bunch of coriander, leaves
    picked, stems finely chopped
2 teaspoons sesame seeds, briefly
    toasted in a hot, dry frying pan

# prawn, asparagus and noodle salad

Combine the sugar, fish sauce, lime juice and vegetable oil and toss the prawns through.

Cook the noodles according to the instructions on the packet, drain and refresh under cold water.

Cook the asparagus in boiling salted water for 3–5 minutes (depending on thickness) until just tender, drain and refresh under cold water. Combine the asparagus with the cucumber, radishes and noodles. Add the chilli, garlic, spring onions and coriander stems.

Add the prawn mixture to the noodles and toss everything so it is well coated. Serve with a generous sprinkling of the reserved coriander leaves and sesame seeds.

*If you buy raw prawns for a salad like this, it is best to cook the prawns gently, starting them in cold salted water, bringing them to the boil and simmering for a couple of minutes, before draining and peeling. This way the flesh stays moist and succulent.*

# seafood salad
# with wilted greens

serves 2

for the dressing

1 tablespoon toasted sesame oil

2 tablespoons soy sauce

½ teaspoon sugar

2 tablespoons rice vinegar

2 spring onions, finely sliced

3cm piece of ginger root, peeled
and grated

2 garlic cloves, peeled and minced
with a little salt

100g cellophane noodles

1 head little gem lettuce, trimmed
and shredded

small handful of mangetout, thinly
sliced lengthways

small handful of beansprouts

¼ cucumber, deseeded and
julienned

1 tablespoon vegetable oil

4 scallops, trimmed (if large, slice
horizontally)

4 raw, peeled prawns

8 clams, well rinsed and drained

handful of spinach

bunch of coriander, leaves picked

Soak the noodles according to the instructions on the packet, drain and refresh under cold water. Roughly chop and put in a large bowl.

Combine the dressing ingredients and stir to dissolve the sugar. Add to the bowl with the lettuce, mangetout, beansprouts and cucumber, toss well and check the seasoning. Heat the oil in a hot wok over a medium heat and stir fry the scallops, prawns and clams for 2 minutes until cooked and the clams are open.

Add the spinach, wilt briefly over the heat and add everything to the salad bowl. Toss well, adding in the coriander as you go, and serve.

# kamaboko-aka salad

serves 2

100g cellophane noodles

1 whole red *kamaboko-aka* (see
page 11), sliced

1 stick celery, thinly sliced

1 tablespoon finely sliced shallots

handful of beansprouts

1 head little gem lettuce, leaves
separated

1 teaspoon fish sauce (*nam pla*)

1 teaspoon soy sauce

salt and white pepper

Cook the noodles according to the instructions on the packet, drain and refresh under cold water.

Combine the *kamaboko-aka*, celery, shallots, beansprouts, lettuce, noodles, fish sauce and soy sauce. Season with salt and pepper and toss well before serving.

# somen noodle salad with scallops and kamaboko-aka

serves 2

for the dressing
125ml soy sauce
125ml rice vinegar
1 teaspoon toasted sesame oil
1 teaspoon sugar

100g *somen* noodles
1 head little gem lettuce, trimmed
    and shredded
½ cucumber, cut into strips using a
    vegetable peeler
½ red pepper, sliced lengthways
1 sheet of *nori* seaweed, cut into
    1cm strips
2 spring onions, finely sliced
1 tablespoon vegetable oil
6 scallops, sliced in half horizontally
½ *kamaboko-aka* (see page 11),
    cut into 2mm slices
1 teaspoon sesame seeds, briefly
    toasted in a hot, dry frying pan

Combine the dressing ingredients in a small bowl.

Cook the noodles according to the instructions on the packet, drain and refresh under cold water.

Combine half the dressing (keep the rest in the fridge for other salads or to serve over noodle dishes; it will last a week or so) with the lettuce, cucumber, red pepper, *nori,* spring onions and noodles and toss well. Transfer to a plate.

Heat the oil in a hot wok. Season the scallops and fry for 1–2 minutes until cooked through. Place on top of the salad ingredients along with the *kamaboko-aka* slices and a sprinkling of sesame seeds.

# prawn and rice vermicelli salad

serves 2

100g rice vermicelli
200g raw, peeled prawns
3cm piece of ginger root, peeled
    and grated
2 garlic cloves, peeled and minced
1 tablespoon fish sauce (*nam pla*)
2 tablespoons vegetable oil
bunch of chives, cut into 6cm
    lengths
1 red chilli, finely chopped
handful of beansprouts
2 tablespoons sweet *miso* dressing
    (see page 23)
bunch of coriander, leaves picked
1 tablespoon sesame seeds, briefly
    toasted in a hot, dry frying pan

Cook the vermicelli according to the instructions on the packet, drain and refresh under cold water.

Toss the prawns with the ginger, garlic and fish sauce.

Heat the oil in a hot wok over a medium heat, add the prawn mixture and stir fry for 2–3 minutes or until the prawns are cooked. Add the noodles, chives, chilli and beansprouts and immediately remove from the heat.

Stir in the sweet *miso* dressing and serve topped with the coriander leaves and sesame seeds.

# mango, prawn and crab noodle salad

serves 2

for the dressing
3cm piece of ginger root, peeled
    and grated
2 garlic cloves, peeled and sliced
juice of 1 lime
1 tablespoon vegetable oil
½ teaspoon sugar
1 tablespoon fish sauce (*nam pla*)
1 tablespoon soy sauce

100g rice noodles
1 mango, peeled and roughly
    chopped
2 tablespoons cooked white
    crabmeat
150g cooked, peeled prawns
small bunch of mint, leaves roughly
    chopped

Cook the noodles according to the instructions on the packet, drain and refresh under cold water.

Combine the dressing ingredients in a large bowl. Mix in the noodles and toss to ensure that everything is well combined.

Stir in the mango, crabmeat, prawns and mint, check the seasoning, and serve.

# marinated sea bass salad

serves 2

100g cellophane noodles
250g sea bass fillets, skinned
1 tablespoon vegetable oil
salt
2 tablespoons *tori kara age* sauce
    (see page 21)
leaves of 1 little gem lettuce
handful of beansprouts
3 spring onions, finely sliced
handful of baby spinach
¼ cucumber, deseeded and
    julienned
1 tablespoon chopped mint leaves
1 garlic clove, peeled and thinly
    sliced
2cm piece of ginger root, peeled
    and julienned
1 tablespoon soy sauce
1 lime, halved

Soak the noodles according to the instructions on the packet, drain and refresh under cold water.

Cut the sea bass into bite-sized pieces. Toss with the oil, season with salt and cook under a hot grill for 3–4 minutes or until just cooked. Remove and transfer to a bowl. Add the *tori kara age* sauce and set aside for 5 minutes.

Combine the noodles, lettuce, beansprouts, spring onions, spinach, cucumber, mint, garlic, ginger and soy sauce in a large bowl. Toss to ensure that everything is well combined and divide between 2 bowls. Top with the fish and its sauce and serve with a lime half.

# warm chicken teriyaki salad

serves 2

**for the marinade**

2 tablespoons sake

2 tablespoons *mirin* (see page 11)

2 tablespoons soy sauce

1 teaspoon light brown sugar

3cm piece of ginger root, peeled
	and grated

2 garlic cloves, peeled and finely
	chopped

200g dark chicken meat (leg or
	thigh), roughly chopped

100g rice vermicelli

2 teaspoons toasted sesame oil

1 tablespoon vegetable oil

2 handfuls of beansprouts

1 head little gem lettuce, leaves
	separated and shredded

1 red chilli, deseeded and finely
	chopped

4 tablespoons frozen peas,
	defrosted

bunch of coriander, leaves picked

salt and white pepper

1 tablespoon coarsely chopped
	salted peanuts

Combine the marinade ingredients in a pan and gently heat to dissolve the sugar. Allow to cool completely then combine with the chicken. Set aside for 1 hour; overnight in the fridge is even better.

Cook the vermicelli according to the instructions on the packet, drain and refresh under cold water. Toss with the sesame oil.

Heat the oil in a hot wok over a medium heat and add the chicken and its marinade. Cook for about 4 minutes until the meat is done and the liquid is reduced and thickened. Remove from the heat.

Combine the noodles with the beansprouts, lettuce, chilli, peas and coriander leaves. Season with salt and pepper and toss to ensure that everything is well mixed.

Pile on to 2 plates, spoon over the chicken and its juices and serve topped with the peanuts.

# chicken sesame noodles

serves 2

100g medium egg noodles
1 tablespoon toasted sesame oil

for the dressing
2 garlic cloves
1cm piece of ginger root, peeled
    and grated
1 tablespoon toasted sesame oil
1 tablespoon soy sauce
1 tablespoon rice vinegar
1 teaspoon Chinese black vinegar
    (available from Oriental stores)
1 teaspoon light brown sugar

100g cooked chicken breast, cut
    into finger-sized strips
½ cucumber, cut lengthways into
    strips using a vegetable peeler
4 radishes, sliced
2 handfuls of beansprouts
2 spring onions, thinly sliced
1 tablespoon sesame seeds, briefly
    toasted in a hot, dry frying pan

Cook the noodles according to the instructions on the packet, drain and refresh under cold water. Toss with the sesame oil and set aside.

Combine the dressing ingredients in a large bowl and stir in the chicken.

Toss the chicken and dressing with the noodles and scatter over the cucumber, radishes, beansprouts, spring onions and sesame seeds.

serves 2

100g French beans, trimmed and
    cut into 4cm lengths
1 red pepper, deseeded and thinly
    sliced
2 skinless, boneless chicken
    breasts
100g rice noodles
juice of 2 limes
2 teaspoons light soft brown sugar
2 tablespoons soy sauce
50g fresh mango, cut into 1cm
    cubes
small bunch of mint, leaves
    picked and roughly chopped
60g roasted, salted peanuts,
    roughly chopped
salt and white pepper

# chicken and mango rice noodle salad

Bring a large pan of salted water to the boil, cook the beans for about 4 minutes, or until just tender. Add the red pepper and return to the boil. Lift out immediately using a slotted spoon and refresh under cold water. Drain well and set aside.

Slide the chicken breasts into the same pan of boiling water, reduce the heat and simmer for 6–8 minutes or until cooked. Remove the chicken and allow to cool. Slice into bite-sized pieces.

Add the noodles to the boiling water and cook according to the instructions on the packet, drain and refresh under cold water.

In a large bowl, whisk together the lime juice and sugar until the sugar dissolves, then add the soy sauce. Stir in the vegetables, noodles, chicken, mango and mint.

Season with salt and pepper and toss everything lightly to dress all the ingredients. Taste and adjust the seasoning as required.

Serve with the peanuts scattered over the top.

serves 2

100g *somen* noodles
2 teaspoons tahini paste
3cm piece of ginger root, peeled
    and grated
1 small jalapeño chilli, deseeded
    and finely chopped
2 teaspoons soy sauce
2 teaspoons rice vinegar
1 tablespoon vegetable oil
salt and white pepper
100g boneless chicken thigh meat,
    roughly chopped
1 head little gem lettuce, leaves
    finely shredded
½ cucumber, cut lengthways into
    strips using a vegetable peeler
handful of mint leaves
handful of coriander leaves

# chicken and coriander somen noodles

Cook the noodles according to the instructions on the packet, drain and refresh under cold water.

Combine the tahini paste, ginger and chilli with the soy sauce and rice vinegar in a small bowl.

Heat the oil in a hot wok, season the chicken and stir fry until golden brown and cooked through. Add the tahini sauce and stir in 2 tablespoons warm water. Combine the chicken, sauce, noodles, lettuce, cucumber, mint and coriander. Check the seasoning and serve.

# marinated duck salad

serves 2

for the marinade

1 teaspoon rice vinegar

1 teaspoon honey

1 teaspoon soy sauce

1 duck breast, sliced on the
    diagonal

1 tablespoon vegetable oil

200g *somen* noodles

bunch of spring onions, sliced
    lengthways

½ cucumber, deseeded and
    julienned

1 carrot, julienned

2 tablespoons hoisin sauce

salt and white pepper

2 teaspoons sesame seeds, briefly
    toasted in a hot, dry frying pan

Combine the marinade ingredients in a small pan with 100ml cold water, bring to the boil and remove from the heat as soon as the honey has melted. Allow to cool completely and pour over the duck slices. Toss gently and set aside for 1 hour; overnight in the fridge is even better.

Pour the marinade off the duck and discard. Heat the oil in a hot wok and stir fry the duck for 3–4 minutes until cooked. Set aside.

Cook the noodles according to the instructions on the packet, drain and refresh under cold water.

Combine the noodles with the spring onions, cucumber, carrot and hoisin sauce in a large bowl. Add the duck and toss everything gently so it is well mixed and coated. Season to taste with salt and pepper.

Serve topped with the sesame seeds.

# chicken noodle salad

serves 2

50g rice vermicelli

1 tablespoon vegetable oil

3cm piece of ginger root, peeled
    and grated

2 teaspoons soy sauce

zest and juice of 1 lime

2 teaspoons toasted sesame oil

75g cooked chicken breast, sliced

1 head little gem lettuce,
    finely sliced

1 red chilli, deseeded and
    finely sliced

2 spring onions, thinly sliced

handful of beansprouts

½ cucumber, deseeded and finely
    sliced

1 tablespoon roughly chopped
    roasted peanuts

handful of coriander leaves

Cook the vermicelli according to the instructions on the packet, drain and refresh under cold water. Roughly chop.

Combine the vegetable oil with the ginger, soy sauce, lime zest and juice and the sesame oil. Toss with the noodles. Stir in the chicken, lettuce, chilli, spring onions, beansprouts and cucumber.

Serve topped with the peanuts and coriander leaves.

2 teaspoons *char siu* sauce
    (Chinese barbecue sauce which
    is widely available)
1 garlic clove, peeled and finely
    chopped
pinch of Chinese five-spice
    (available from Oriental stores)
pinch of ground cinnamon
2 teaspoons sake
2 teaspoons rice vinegar or
    lemon juice

75g pork fillet
2 tablespoons vegetable oil
125g sugar
125ml soy sauce
125ml rice vinegar
100g *somen* noodles
2 eggs, beaten and seasoned
1 head little gem lettuce, finely
    sliced
⅓ cucumber, deseeded and
    thinly sliced
3 spring onions, thinly sliced
    on the diagonal
½ roll *kamaboko-aka* (see page 11),
    cut into 2mm slices
1 sheet of *nori* seaweed, cut
    into strips
salt and white pepper
1 teaspoon toasted sesame oil
½ teaspoon sesame seeds, briefly
    toasted in a hot, dry frying pan
½ teaspoon black sesame seeds

# marinated pork and somen noodle salad

Put the marinade ingredients in a polythene freezer bag, add the pork, massage for a few minutes and transfer to the fridge overnight or for as long as possible.

Preheat the oven to 200°C/gas mark 6. Heat a heavy-bottomed frying pan until hot, add 1 tablespoon of the vegetable oil and put the pork in for 2–3 minutes to seal, rolling it around until golden all over. Transfer to a roasting tray and roast for 20 minutes or until cooked. Remove and rest for 5 minutes, then cut into discs 5mm thick.

Combine the sugar, soy sauce and rice vinegar and stir to dissolve the sugar. This is the dressing.

Cook the noodles according to the instructions on the packet, drain and refresh under cold water.

Heat the remaining oil in a hot wok then add the egg, swirl around so that it thinly coats the bottom of the wok and cook until set, about 1 minute. Remove, allow to cool, then roll up and thinly slice.

To serve, mix together the pork, noodles, egg strips, lettuce, cucumber, spring onions, *kamaboko-aka* and *nori* and place in a serving bowl. Whisk the dressing and pour over 3 tablespoons (the remainder can be stored in an airtight container in the fridge for a few weeks). Toss to ensure that everything is well mixed, season with salt and pepper, drizzle over the sesame oil and serve with a sprinkling of the sesame seeds.

wagamama

# drinks

What to drink with noodles is something of a challenge. Consider it more to do with preference than anything else, as noodles are pretty easy really. Tea is popular. Green is favourite, but there is nothing wrong with a straight cuppa if that is what you prefer. Many opt for beer — we favour Japanese beers in the restaurants. Juices and smoothies get high marks from customers; it's a health thing. But also a taste thing. Wine works well, although you need to be a little cautious with the spicier dishes and those where the chilli factor is higher, as some wines are more suited than others. Red or white is a matter of choice. Noodles seem to like both. Sake is well worth considering, of which more later. And plain water is rather delicious, ice-cold it is refreshing and very complementary to a slurp or two. Of noodles as well as of water.

# juices and smoothies

Sales of juices and smoothies have increased significantly in recent years, not just at wagamama but generally. Packed with clean pure flavours, the health benefits seem like a bonus point. Some of these drinks are almost like a meal in themselves, which is partly why they sit at the top of the menu. A glass of raw juice (carrot, cucumber, tomato, orange and apple) is a great way to enjoy the anticipation of a bowl of noodles.

Apart from orange and grapefruit juice, juices are not that easy to produce at home unless you have a proper juice machine. This pulps the fruit or vegetable in order to extract the juice. Smoothies are somewhat easier, although you do have to stick to softer ingredients, like bananas, mangoes and berries. Most smoothies contain banana, which helps to give the drink some body. There really is no end to the variations of juices possible.

What follows are a couple of suggestions that make use of a blender. If you decide to purchase a juicer the whole world of vegetables adds a completely different dimension.

## orange, lychee, grape and mint juice

serves 1

1 orange, peeled, deseeded and all white pith removed
20 seedless red grapes
10 lychees, tinned or fresh
10 sprigs of mint

Place everything in a blender or food processor and blitz on the pulse setting until smooth. Serve immediately.

## banana, pear, honey and lime smoothie

serves 1

1 small banana, peeled
1 pear, peeled and cored
1 lime, peeled and all white pith removed
2 teaspoons honey

Place everything in a blender or food processor and blitz on the pulse setting until smooth. Serve immediately.

# water

If you opt for spicier dishes it might be worth avoiding sparkling water as the bubbles tend to accentuate the chilli burn. A still water, from the tap even, preferably chilled, does much to quench thirst and clear the palate.

# tea

We favour green tea over black. It's the tannins really, which in black tea tend to overpower the noodles, if not all the other ingredients. Jasmin is generally overwhelmed by the food. Which leaves green tea sitting rather neatly in the middle. In the world of green teas there are literally hundreds to choose from. To those in the know there are also huge differences. Best to try and see which one you prefer.

**serves 2**

250g cooked rice
100g cooked fish, loosely flaked
500ml green tea
1 sheet *nori* seaweed, roughly torn

# tea and rice

Pour the tea over the rice and fish, scatter the *nori* on top and drink/eat/slurp.

*This is a popular way of finishing a meal in Japan: tea is poured over leftover rice to make a kind of instant porridge. There is a temptation to add other things, as evidenced by the fish in this recipe. A frugal and rather different approach to leftovers.*

**serves 1**

1cm piece of lemongrass, bashed
1 teaspoon peeled and grated
    fresh ginger root
2 teaspoons honey

# lemongrass, ginger and honey infusion

Combine all the ingredients in a small jug and pour over a mug of hot water. Allow to infuse for 5 minutes, strain and serve.

# CHOYA SAKE

THE REFINED
JAPANESE SAKE

SMOOTH
AND DRY

蝶矢

チョーヤ 清酒

CHOYA SAKE CO., LTD. OSAKA JAPAN

NET CONT. 72cl

ALCOHOL CONTENT: 13.5% Vol.

PRODUCE OF JAPAN

# wine

If it's white you want, stick to something dry, fairly neutral and fresh (which means a generous but balanced acidity). Aromatic whites are also worth considering. Grape varieties to look out for include Sauvignon Blanc, Pinot Gris, Pinot Blanc, Riesling and Viognier.

On the red side, watch out for tannins which come up hard against chillies and anything spicy. Light and fresh is the favoured route: Beaujolais, Syrah (provided the tannins are low), wines from the Loire – Chinon, for example – or light Sangiovese and Tempranillo.

Rosé may be a pretty general term in that the wines vary hugely, but on the whole they partner really well, their light fruitiness working harmoniously with the spiciness and the absence of tannins avoiding any clash.

# beer

Beer is not quite as easy or obvious as it might at first seem. We have Japanese beers on the menu because they are dry, not too hoppy and not overly gassy, which makes them good partners with food. They also have some character which is necessary for them to stand up to the food. Avoid inexpensive lagers, which tend to fall at the first post. But look out for the more interesting lagers which tend to have bags of character and sufficient alcohol (around 5% abv) to cope with the flavours. The darker beers – ales, porters and stouts – tend to overwhelm the more delicate aspects of the food.

# sake

Sake's body, character, aroma and strength make it very suited to combining with this kind of food. Like fino or manzanilla sherry (both of which are worth trying with noodles) sake is able to handle the chilli and spicy notes well. There are many sakes and price is not necessarily a straight indication of, or route to, satisfaction. On the menu we have two, one slightly sweeter than the other. If you are buying a bottle the labelling has become a lot clearer than it used to be. Look out for *nihonshu-do*, an indication of dryness and sweetness. +15 is very dry, −15 is very sweet with neutral being between −3 and +5. *Sanmi-do* refers to the acidity, from 0.6 in light sake to 2.8 for heavier sake. Serve warm or cold? This is really a matter of personal preference. If you prefer it warm, as we do, pour it into a heatproof jug and place in a pan of water over a gentle heat, but be careful not to let it boil.

## oven temperatures

| Celsius* | Fahrenheit | Gas | Description |
| --- | --- | --- | --- |
| 110°C | 225°F | mark ¼ | cool |
| 130°C | 250°F | mark ½ | cool |
| 140°C | 275°F | mark 1 | very low |
| 150°C | 300°F | mark 2 | very low |
| 170°C | 325°F | mark 3 | low |
| 180°C | 350°F | mark 4 | moderate |
| 190°C | 375°F | mark 5 | moderate-hot |
| 200°C | 400°F | mark 6 | hot |
| 220°C | 425°F | mark 7 | hot |
| 230°C | 450°F | mark 8 | very hot |

\* For fan-assisted ovens, reduce temperatures by 10°C

## volume

| | |
| --- | --- |
| 5ml | 1 teaspoon |
| 10ml | 1 dessert spoon |
| 15ml | 1 tablespoon |
| 30ml | 1fl oz |
| 50ml | 2fl oz |
| 75ml | 3fl oz |
| 100ml | 3½fl oz |
| 125ml | 4fl oz |
| 150ml | 5fl oz (¼ pint) |
| 200ml | 7fl oz (⅓ pint) |
| 250ml (¼ litre) | 9fl oz |
| 300ml | 10fl oz (½ pint) |
| 350ml | 12fl oz |
| 400ml | 14fl oz |
| 425ml | 15fl oz (¾ pint) |
| 450ml | 16fl oz |
| 500ml (½ litre) | 18fl oz |
| 600ml | 1 pint (20fl oz) |
| 700ml | 1¼ pints |
| 850ml | 1½ pints |
| 1 litre | 1¾ pints |
| 1.2 litres | 2 pints |
| 1.5 litres | 2½ pints |
| 1.8 litres | 3 pints |
| 2 litres | 3½ pints |

## weight

| | |
| --- | --- |
| 10g | ½oz |
| 20g | ¾oz |
| 25g | 1oz |
| 50g | 2oz |
| 60g | 2½oz |
| 75g | 3oz |
| 100g | 3½oz |
| 110g | 4oz (¼lb) |
| 150g | 5oz |
| 175g | 6oz |
| 200g | 7oz |
| 225g | 8oz (½lb) |
| 250g (¼kg) | 9oz |
| 275g | 10oz |
| 350g | 12oz (¾lb) |
| 400g | 14oz |
| 450g | 1lb |
| 500g (½kg) | 18oz |
| 600g | 1¼lb |
| 700g | 1½lb |
| 900g | 2lb |
| 1kg | 2¼lb |
| 1.1kg | 2½lb |
| 1.3kg | 3lb |
| 1.5kg | 3lb 5oz |
| 1.6kg | 3½lb |
| 1.8kg | 4lb |
| 2kg | 4½lb |
| 2.2kg | 5lb |

## measurements

| | |
| --- | --- |
| 3mm | ⅛in |
| 5mm | ¼in |
| 1cm | ½in |
| 2cm | ¾in |
| 2.5cm | 1in |
| 3cm | 1¼in |
| 4cm | 1½in |
| 5cm | 2in |
| 6cm | 2½in |
| 7.5cm | 2¾in |
| 9cm | 3½in |
| 10cm | 4in |
| 11.5cm | 4½in |
| 12.5cm | 5in |
| 15cm | 6in |
| 17cm | 6½in |
| 18cm | 7in |
| 20.5cm | 8in |
| 23cm | 9in |
| 24cm | 9½in |
| 25.5cm | 10in |
| 30.5cm | 11in |

# index